AF262744

BOUCHER'S
FOUR SEASONS

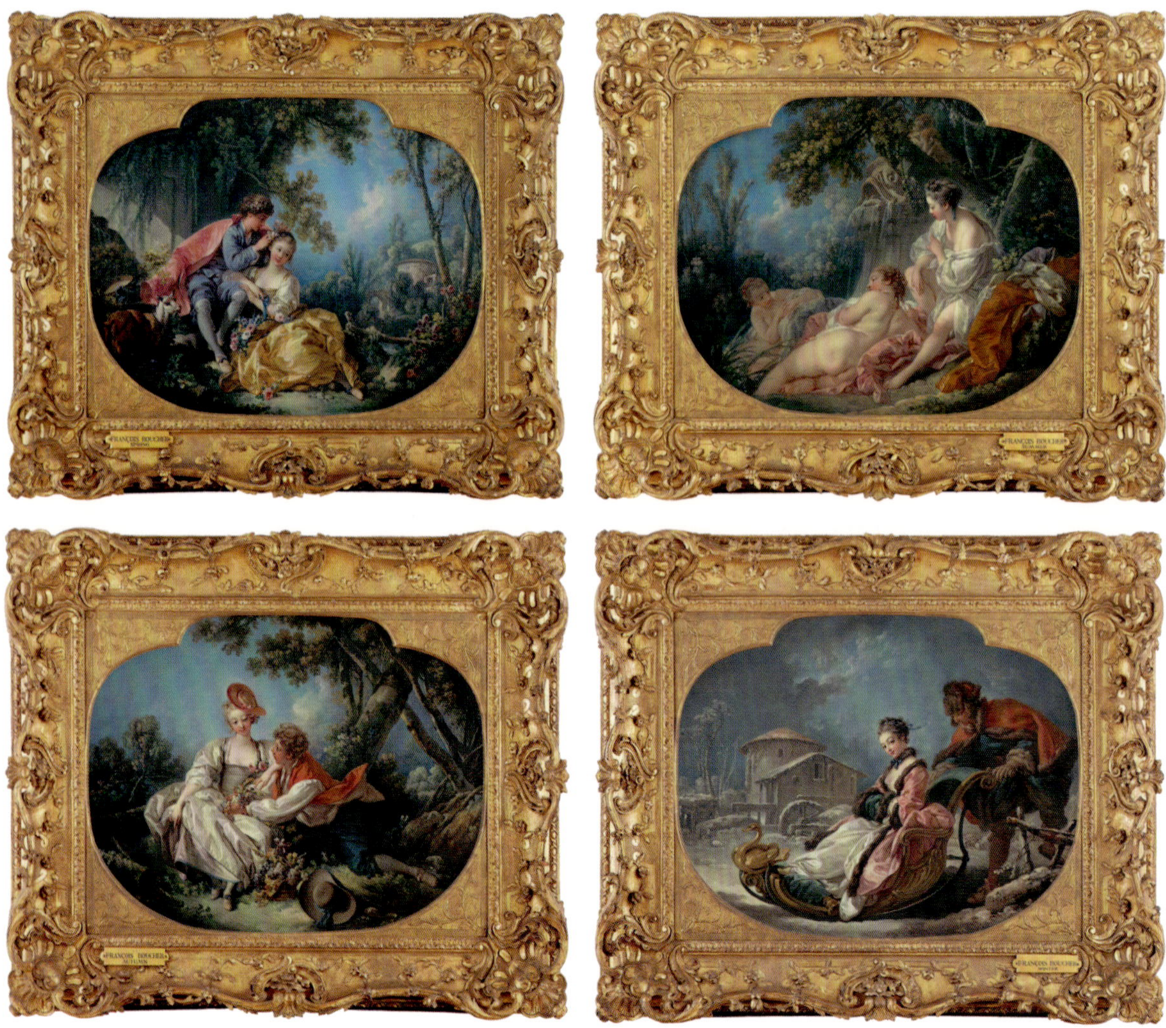

BOUCHER'S FOUR SEASONS

Xavier F. Salomon

Flora Yukhnovich

The Frick Collection, New York
in association with D Giles Limited

FRICK DIPTYCH SERIES

Designed to foster critical engagement and interest specialist and non-specialist alike, each book in this series illuminates a single work in the Frick's rich collection with an essay by a Frick curator paired with a contribution from a contemporary artist or writer.

First published in 2026 by The Frick Collection
1 East 70th Street
New York, NY 10021
www.frick.org

Michaelyn Mitchell, Editor in Chief
Gemma McElroy, Assistant Editor

In association with GILES
An imprint of D Giles Limited
66 High Street
Lewes, BN7 1XG, UK
gilesltd.com

EU GPSR authorised representative
LOGOS EUROPE, 9 rue Nicolas Poussin, 17000,
La Rochelle, France
E-mail: contact@logoseurope.eu

Copyedited and proofread by Sarah Kane
Designed by Caroline and Roger Hillier,
The Old Chapel Graphic Design

Typeset in Garamond
Produced by GILES
Printed and bound in China

A CIP catalogue record for this book is available from the Library of Congress.

ISBN: 978-1-913875-73-2

Cover: Detail from François Boucher, *The Four Seasons: Summer*, 1755. Oil on canvas, 22½ × 28⅝ in. (57.2 × 72.7 cm). The Frick Collection, New York

Frontispiece: François Boucher, *The Four Seasons: Spring, Summer, Autumn,* and *Winter*, 1755. Oil on canvas, each 22½ × 28⅝ in. (57.2 × 72.7 cm). The Frick Collection, New York

Distributed in the USA and Canada by
Consortium Book Sales & Distribution
The Keg House
34 Thirteenth Avenue, NE, Suite 101
Minneapolis, MN 55413-1007
USA
www.cbsd.com

CONTENTS

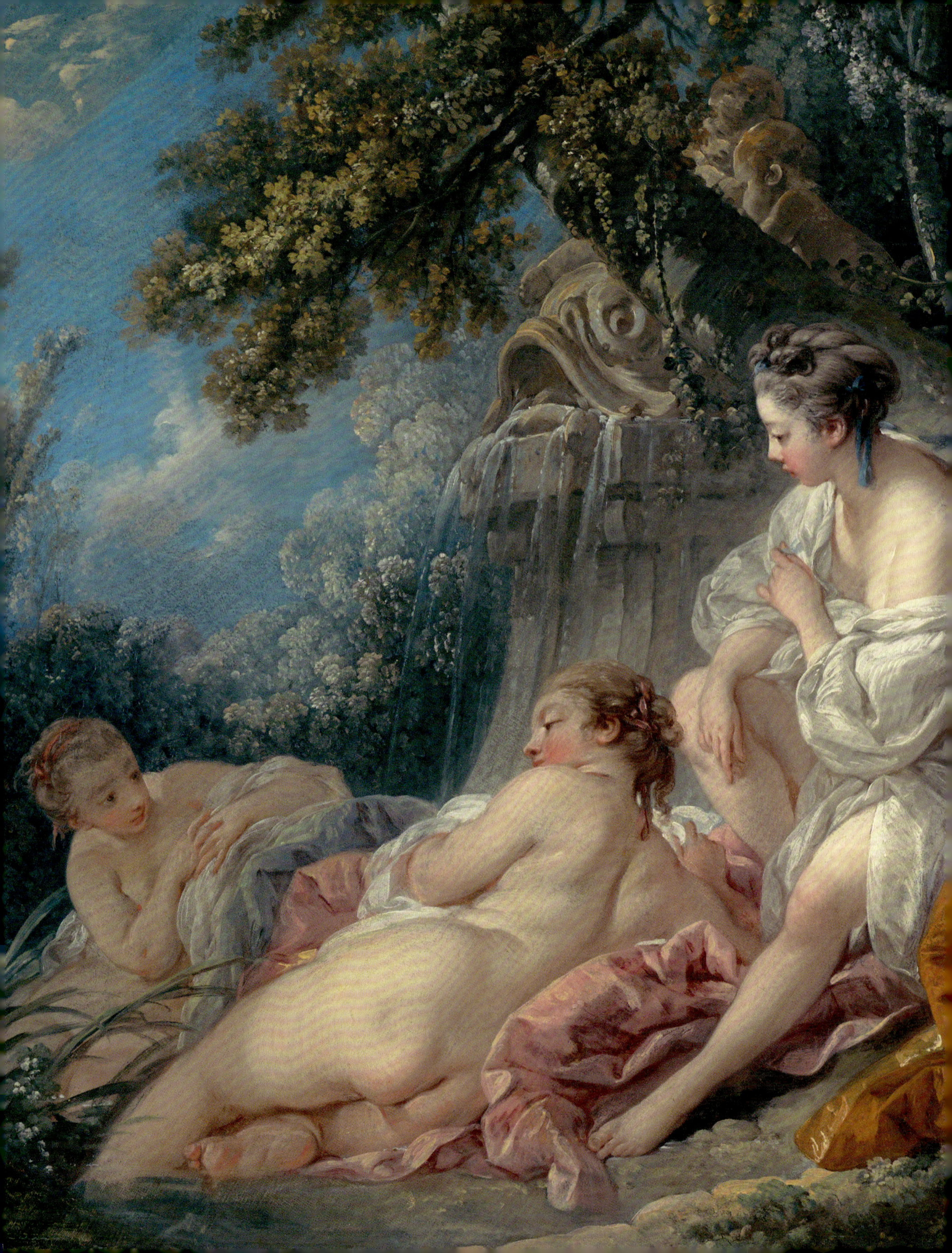

Nineteen sixteen was something of a Boucher year for Henry Clay Frick. In August, he acquired eight canvases by Francois Boucher representing the Arts and Sciences for his wife's boudoir, the so-called Boucher Room; and in October, he purchased *The Four Seasons*, a set of four pastoral scenes commissioned for Madame de Pompadour, Louis XV's official mistress. She represented the epitome of fashion and taste at the French court in the mid-eighteenth century. She was also a great patron of the arts, and she employed the talents of Boucher, a leading artist of his day, to their mutual benefit. Since its acquisition, *The Four Seasons* has lined the walls of the Frick's West Vestibule, the small hallway leading from the Grand Stair to the Fifth Avenue Garden.

In this seventeenth volume of the Frick's celebrated Diptych series, Deputy Director and Peter Jay Sharp Chief Curator Xavier F. Salomon investigates the intricacies of each scene of *The Four Seasons* and traces the paintings' histories, including the evolution of their appearance over the centuries. Paired with Xavier's essay is a text and images of a new work—inspired by *The Four Seasons*— by Flora Yukhnovich. Flora's paintings are a re-exploration of Boucher's themes and colors with an infusion of contemporary references. We are delighted to be able to present Flora's paintings in our Cabinet, and we are most grateful to both Xavier and Flora for their contributions to this publication

Thanks also go to Editor in Chief Michaelyn Mitchell, who coordinated the production of the publication and, with Assistant Editor Gemma McElroy, edited the text. We would also like to express our gratitude to our publishing partner, D Giles Limited. Others to whom we extend our thanks include Tia Chapman, Joseph Coscia Jr., Allison Galea, Lisa Goble, Julia Day, Caitlin Henningsen, Patrick King, George Koelle, Alexis Light, Sara Muskulus, Jenna Nugent, Christopher Roberson, Heidi Rosenau, April Kim Tonin, and Sean Troxell, along with the entire staff of the museum, all of whom played a role in the realization of the book and Yukhnovich installation.

Axel Rüger
Anna-Maria and Stephen Kellen Director
The Frick Collection

ACKNOWLEDGMENTS

While researching and writing the essay for this book, I planned to share a final draft of it with Alastair Laing, the widely respected expert on the work of François Boucher. An inexhaustible and incredibly generous scholar and colleague, Alastair, over the last two decades, provided me with a wealth of information on all art historical subjects, starting in my days as a university student at the Courtauld Institute of Art. Regrettably, he died suddenly in June 2024, so I was never able to discuss the subject of this book with him. I know that my text is poorer for it.

Two fortuitous events in the last four years informed this project. The first was an invitation from Michał Przygoda to attend a performance of Stanisław Moniuszko's opera *Straszny dwór* (The Haunted Manor), at the Great Theatre in Warsaw in January 2020. The recognition that the sets, by Leslie Travers, were inspired by *The Four Seasons* at the Frick prompted me to think about the canvases—often undeservedly eclipsed by the Fragonard and Boucher rooms at the museum—in new ways. The second event was my attendance, in September 2021, at the opening of Doron Langberg's exhibition at the Victoria Miro gallery in London, where I met Flora Yukhnovich. A number of inspiring conversations about Rococo art with Flora, in and outside her studio, led to the commission of her contribution for this Diptych: an extraordinary cycle of paintings inspired by Boucher's *Four Seasons* to be displayed at the Frick, in a space on the first floor, occupied between 1935 and 2020 by the Boucher Room. It has been an honor to work on this project with Flora. I have learned so much by looking at her paintings, in her London and New York studios, at the Wallace Collection (in July 2024), and at Ordrupgaard (in November 2024). My greatest thanks and admiration go to Flora.

At the Frick, I would like to thank Ian Wardropper, the former Anna-Maria and Stephen Kellen Director, for his support over more than a decade of our closely working together. My text for this book has, as always, benefited from the sharp eye and scissors of Editor-in-Chief Michaelyn Mitchell, along with Assistant Editor Gemma McElroy. A singular debt of gratitude goes to Alice Spadini, my indefatigable assistant, who gathered the images for the book and supports me in a multitude of ways. I would also like to thank Emerson Bowyer, Xavier Bray, Marie-Laure Buku Pongo, Joe Coscia, Giulio Dalvit, Allison Galea, Joe Godla, Bailey Keiger, Pat King, Aimee Ng, and Lionel Sauvage. Art historians Neil Jeffares and David Pullins, for whose scholarship I have great regard, have been generous, as they always are, with their time, answering questions and providing me with information and research material. I owe each of them an enormous thank you.

Throughout the seasons of my life—through arduous times and joyful glades—none of this would have been possible without M by my side.

Xavier F. Salomon
Director, Calouste Gulbenkian Museum
Former Deputy Director and Peter Jay Sharp Chief Curator,
The Frick Collection

IT'S A JOLLY HOLIDAY WITH BOUCHER

Flora Yukhnovich

I vividly remember the first time François Boucher pushed open the door to my childhood bedroom. It was spring 2017, and I was studying at the time and searching for ideas at the Wallace Collection in London. I found myself standing in front of the eighteenth-century court painter's works—mythological scenes and pastoral idylls, all peachy skin, flushed cheeks, and frills. In an instant, I was sitting cross-legged on my bedroom floor again, playing with Barbies and peering into Polly Pockets, surrounded by plastic pinks and pastel greens, lost in a miniature world of my own making.

I was hooked. To think that something as distant as eighteenth-century Paris could feel so familiar, nostalgic even. The more I looked, the more I noticed Boucher's fingerprints all around me: in reality TV, in fashion, across the internet. The spectacle and the decadence felt distinctly Rococo. I had found my subject. It felt like a language naturally in step with the act of painting—slippery shapes and sinew molded from lush, unruly material. There's a vulgarity to both the Rococo and paint that I find irresistible, like an overripe peach about to split open.

When I first saw *The Four Seasons* at the Frick, I felt the familiar vertigo of dropping into another dimension. These oddly shaped canvases were likely designed as overdoors—painted portals. Tom Stoppard wasn't wrong when he said, "Every exit is an entry to somewhere else."

Like many paintings in the history of art that represent the four seasons, Boucher's quartet offers a bright and cheery cyclical view of life. But while other artists have chosen to illustrate the theme through rural labors, here we have a passage of time that's less taxing, more titillating. Each vignette shows a fresh-faced couple frolicking in a landscape: in spring, a shepherd boy crowns his mistress with flowers; under the hot summer sun, bare-bottomed women bathe beneath a fountain; come autumn, a shepherdess and her lover share a basket of grapes; and during winter, a bundled-up man pushes an elegantly dressed woman across the ice on a sleigh.

Boucher presents an outside world that's polished and preened. Again and again, he depicts overgrown foliage and farm animals, but, like the shells he obsessively collected and laid out in orderly cases, they're carefully contained. It makes sense when you discover that he also designed costumes and stage sets; together with his friend the playwright Charles-Simon Favart, he contributed to the Opéra-Comique in Paris. Several of his pastoral scenes were inspired by Favart's pantomimes. *The Four Seasons* are tantalizingly theatrical—an intricate production (in four acts) of beautiful actors, ambient lighting, and strategically placed props. Scenes as artificial as a heavily filtered image on Instagram or a highlight reel.

The philosopher and critic Denis Diderot said of Boucher's landscapes: "We're dealing not so much with the pictures of a rational being, as with the dreams of a madman." Maybe, but to me it's precisely Boucher's engagement with the theatrical and artificial that makes the work feel so compelling and timely. Boucher has been in my studio constantly, bridging the gap between the Rococo and contemporary popular culture, as I explore the fuzzy mid-space between past and present, figuration and abstraction, freedom and control.

When I began responding to Boucher's *Four Seasons*, the Disney musical *Mary Poppins* came to mind. Boucher's portals reminded me of Mary and the children leaping into Bert's pavement drawings, landing in a surreal pastoral of musical farm animals. It's a painter's dream. I decided to wrap the entire room in a panoramic wallpaper—a painting that envelops the space in a continuous flow of seasons, something you can truly step into. I discovered that in the nineteenth century panoramic wallpapers were treated in much the same way, displayed in purpose-built rooms for viewers to marvel at, a bit like an early version of cinema.

Wallpapers are curious things. They speak of wonder and escape but also of containment. They reassert the very walls around us. Patterns—flowers, fruit, landscapes—all flatten nature into something contained, something ornamental, ordered, repeatable. It makes me wonder what escapism really offers. Whether you're in a gallery, a living room, or scrolling a screen, at what point does staring at a romanticized landscape start to feel oppressive—a stark reminder that you are, in fact, stuck indoors, shut out of the spectacle? Or is getting lost the spectacle—not a denial of reality but a vital part of it? One moment I'm gazing at a jewel-colored canvas by Boucher, and the next, I'm back in my childhood bedroom, pastel pink, daydreaming of a far-off land, a fantasy that would do Disney proud.

Pages 16–17:
The Four Seasons: Winter and *Spring*

Page 18:
The Four Seasons: Winter (detail)

Page 19:
The Four Seasons: Autumn
Oil on mural cloth
100¾ × 209½ in.
(255.9 × 532.1 cm)

The Four Seasons: Winter
Oil on mural cloth
100¾ × 111½ in.
(255.9 × 283.2 cm)

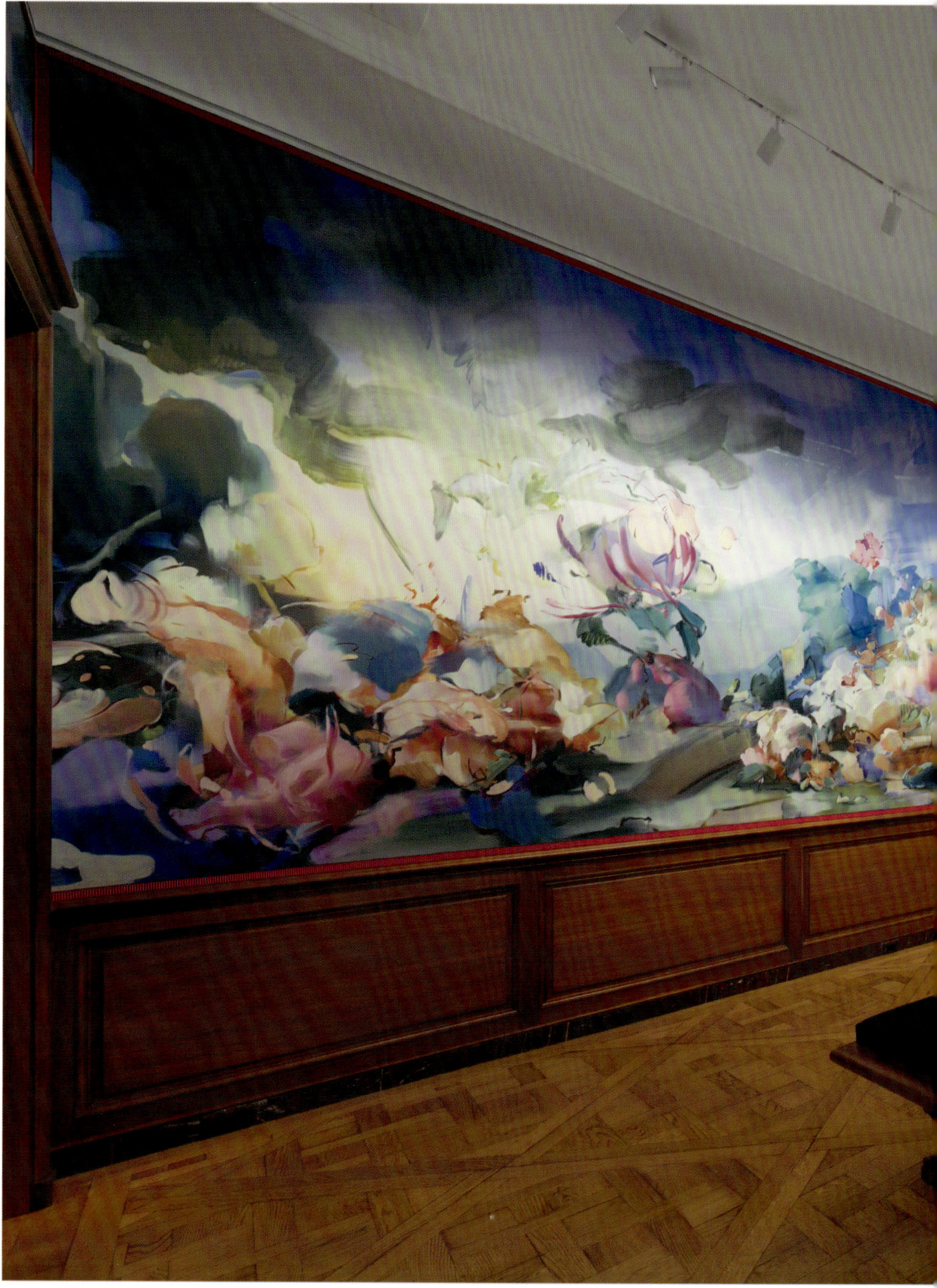

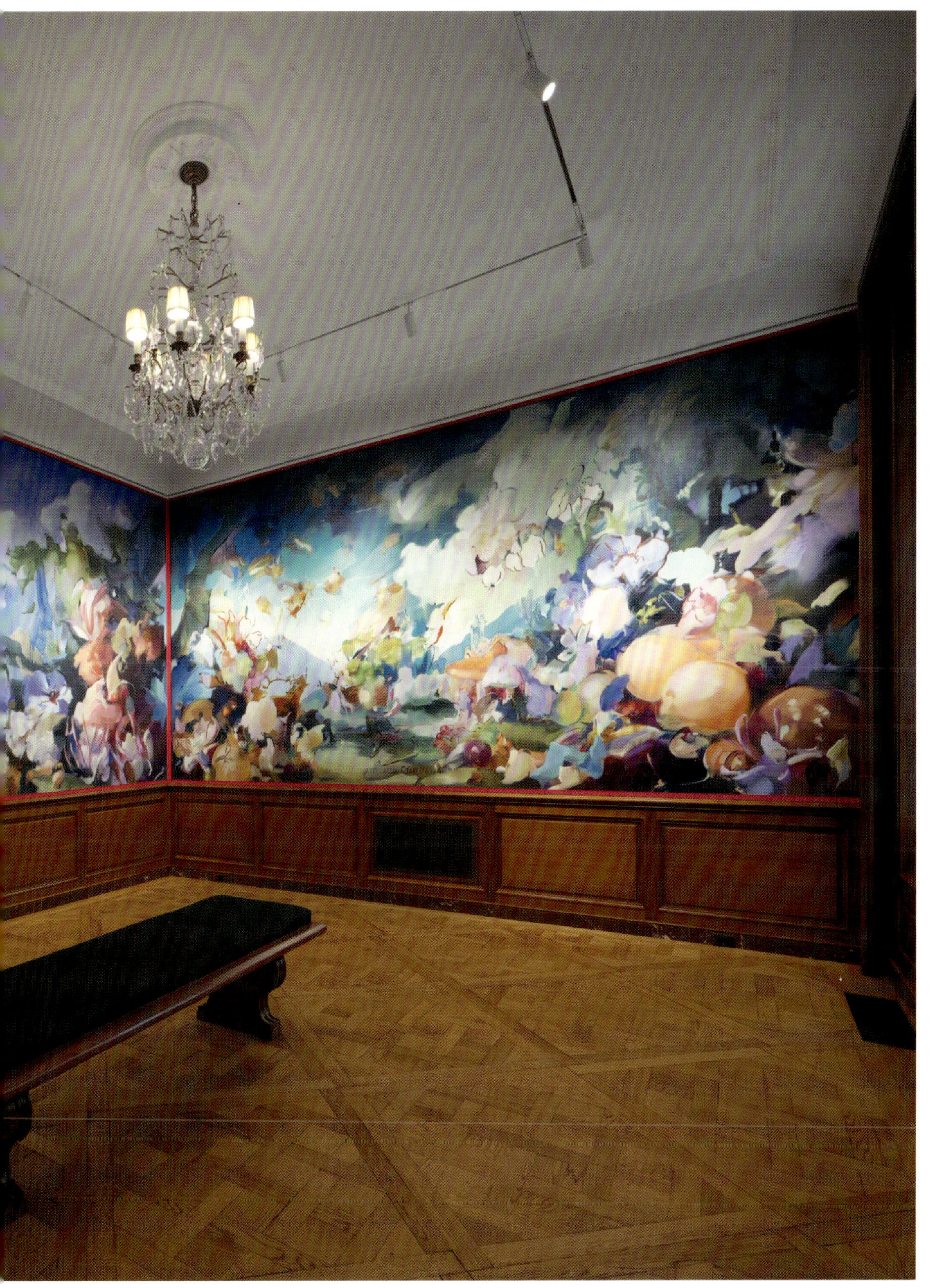

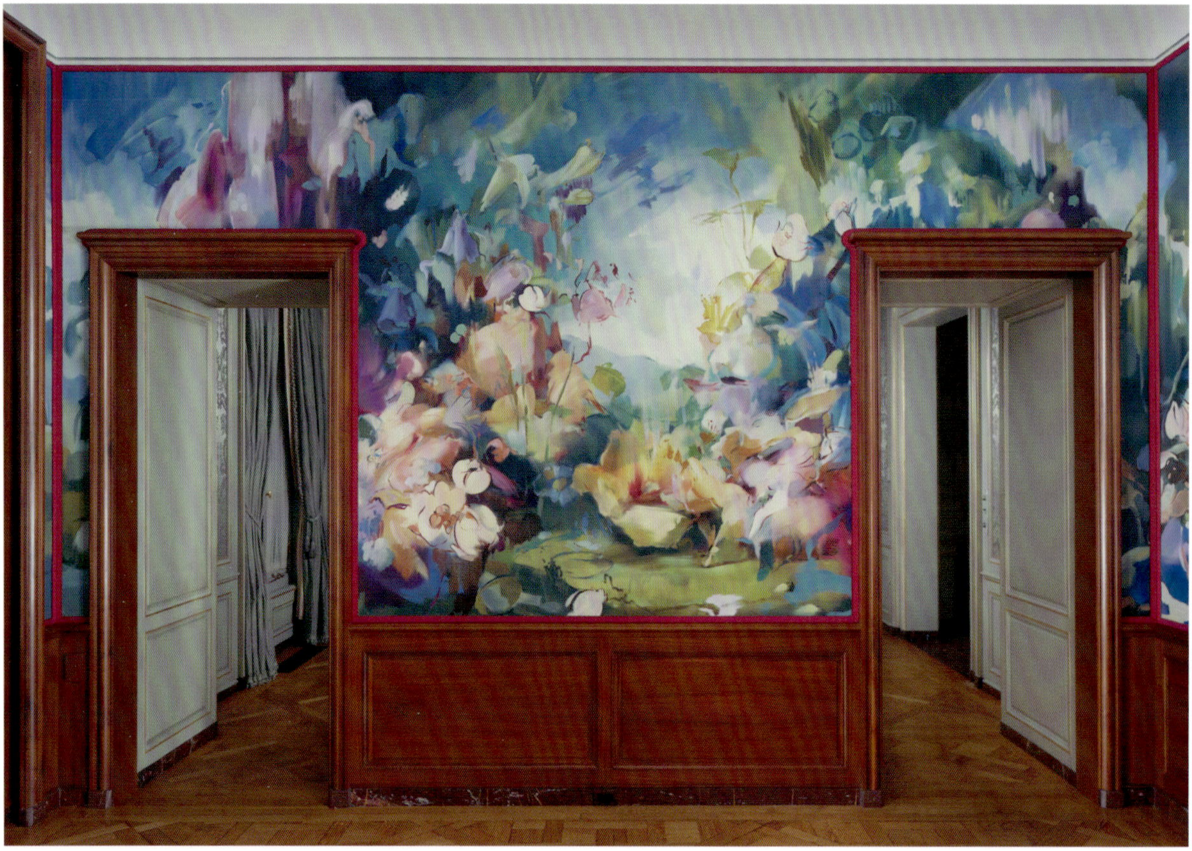

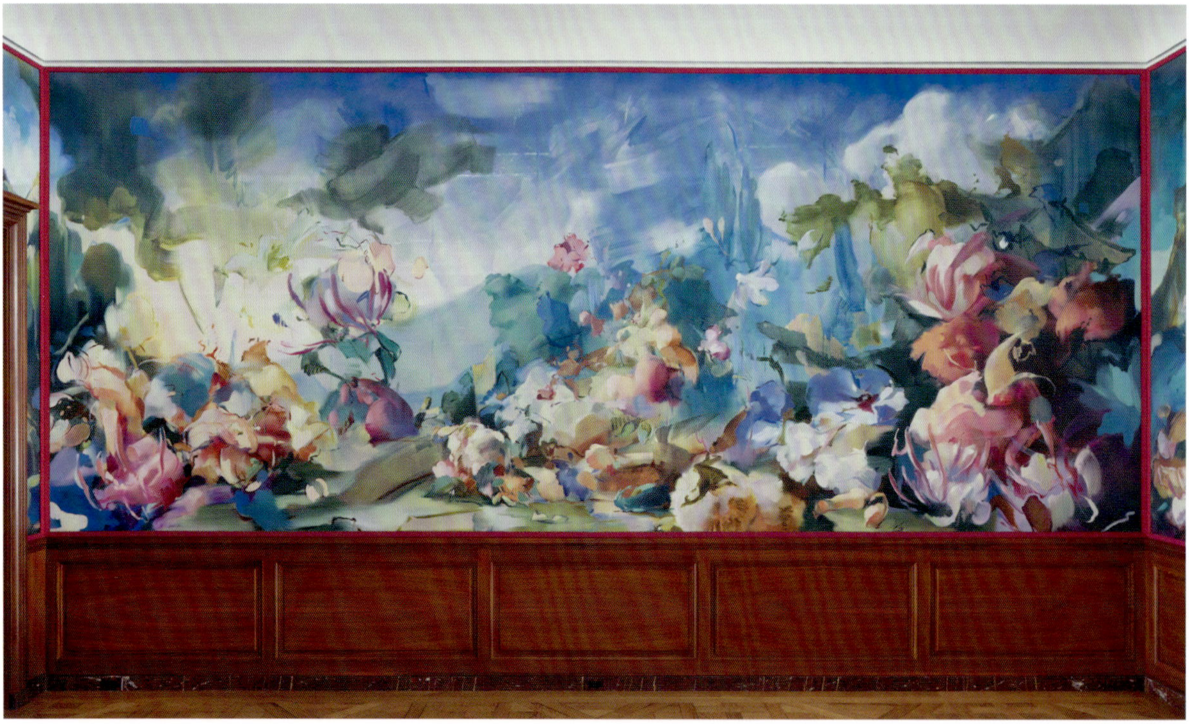

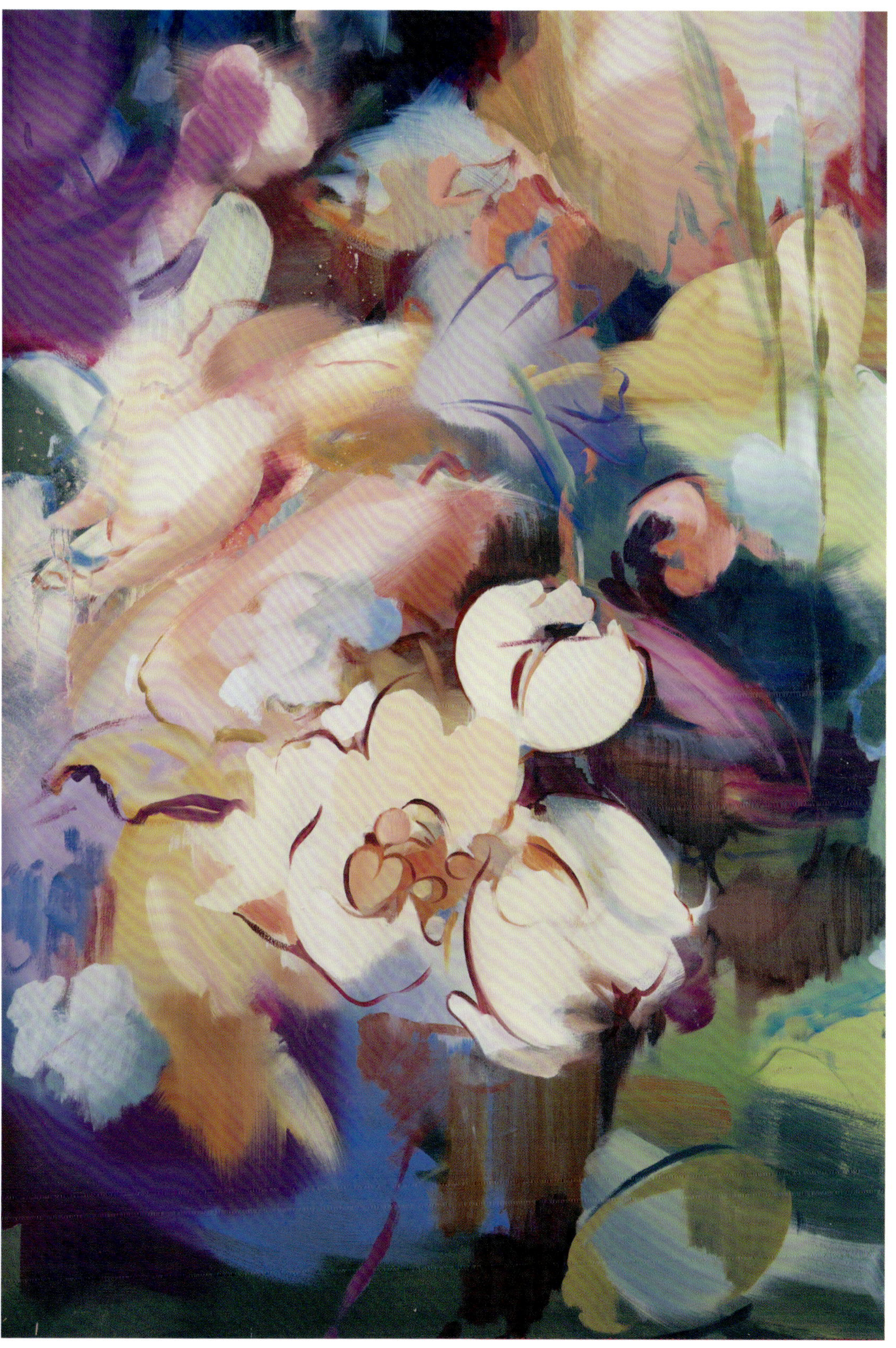

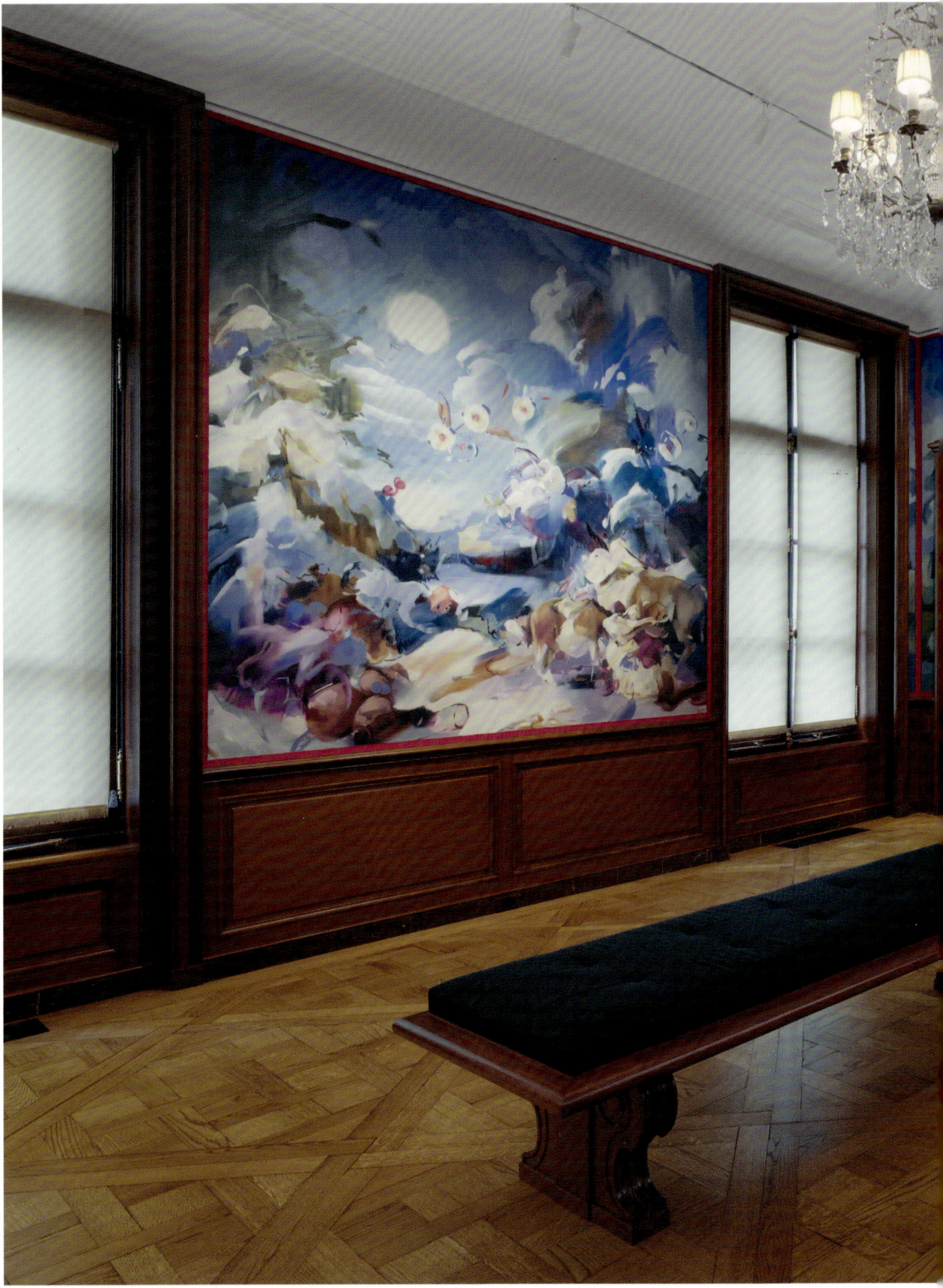

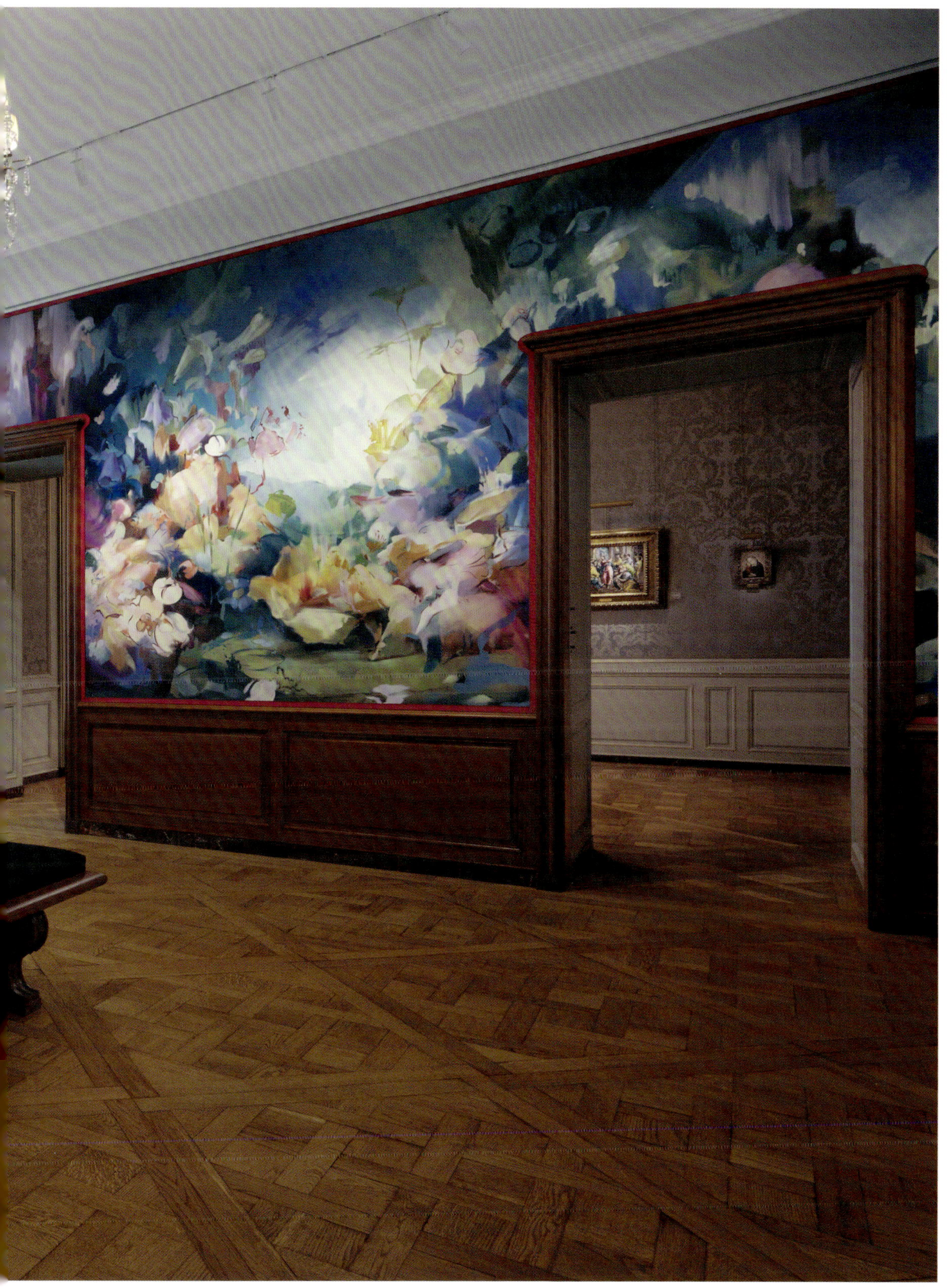

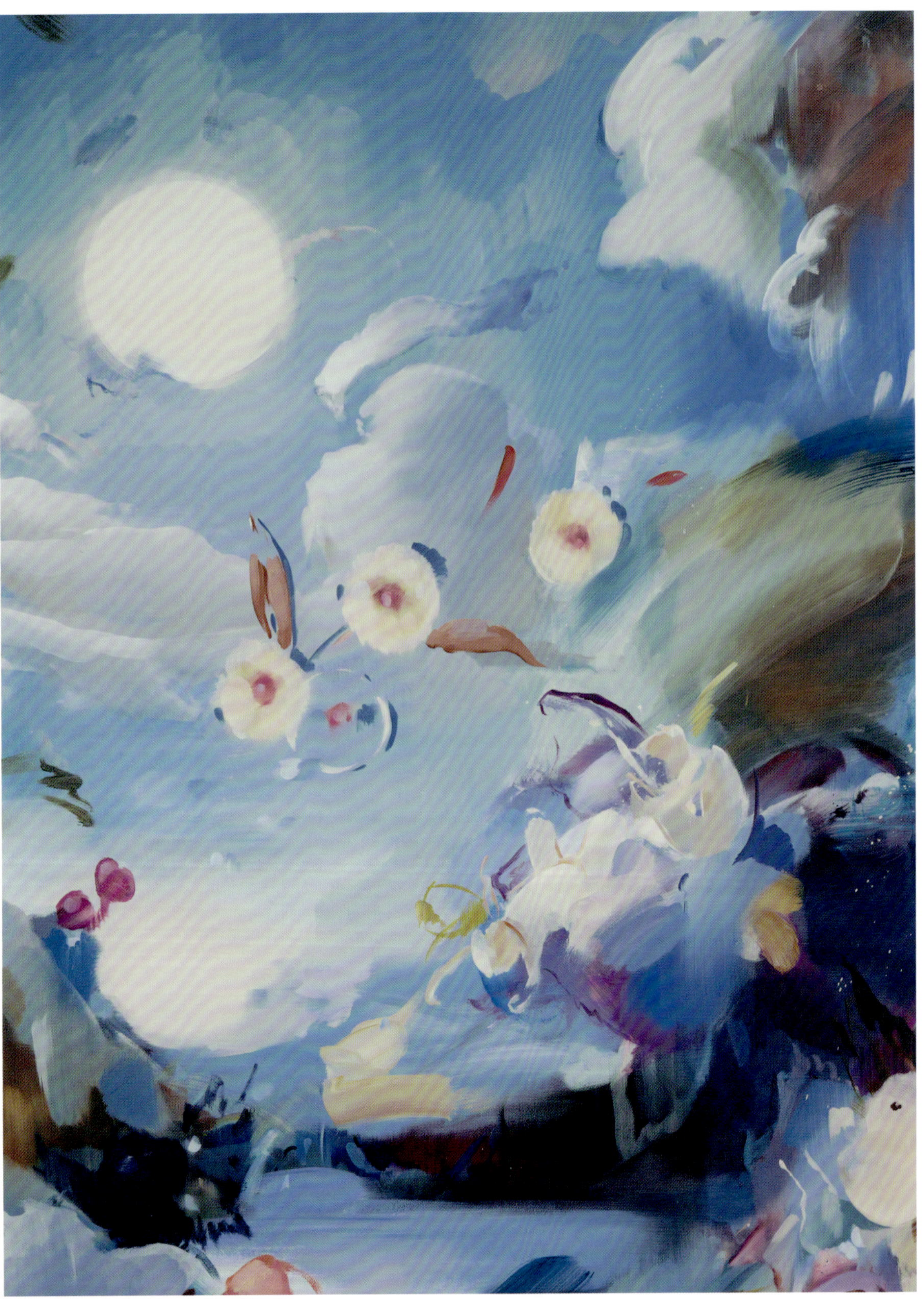

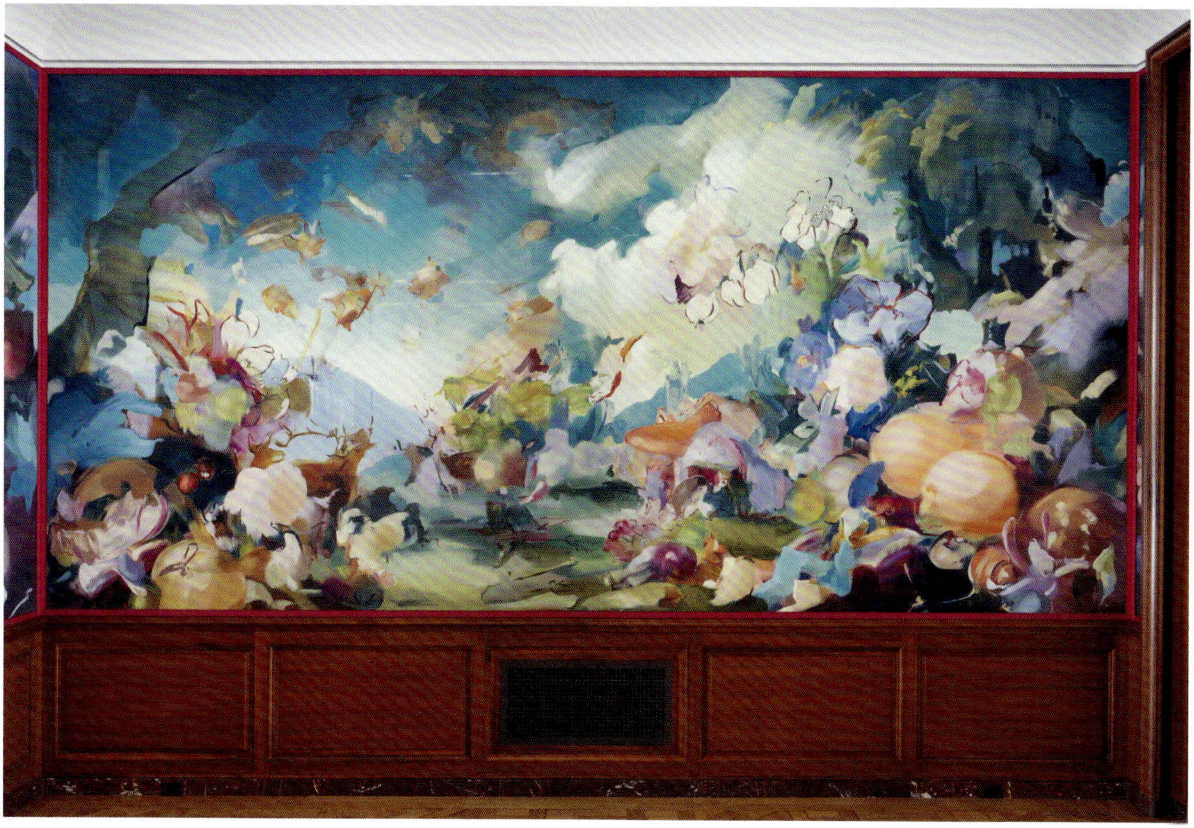

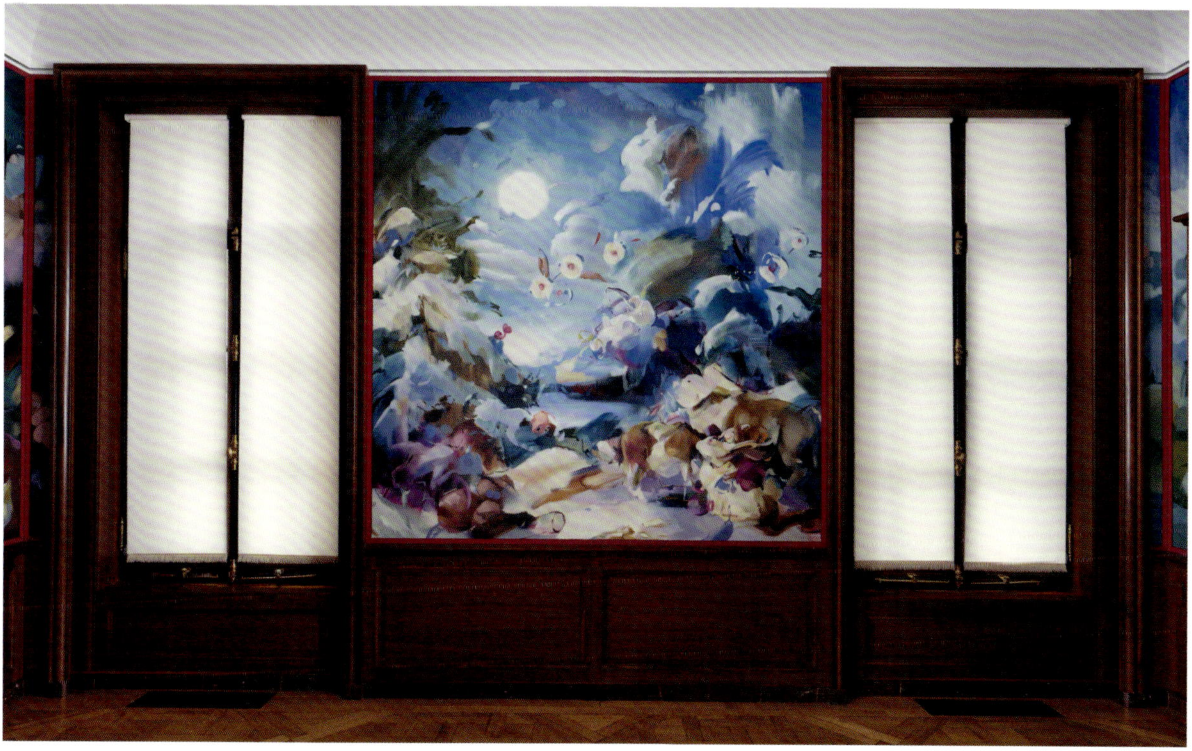

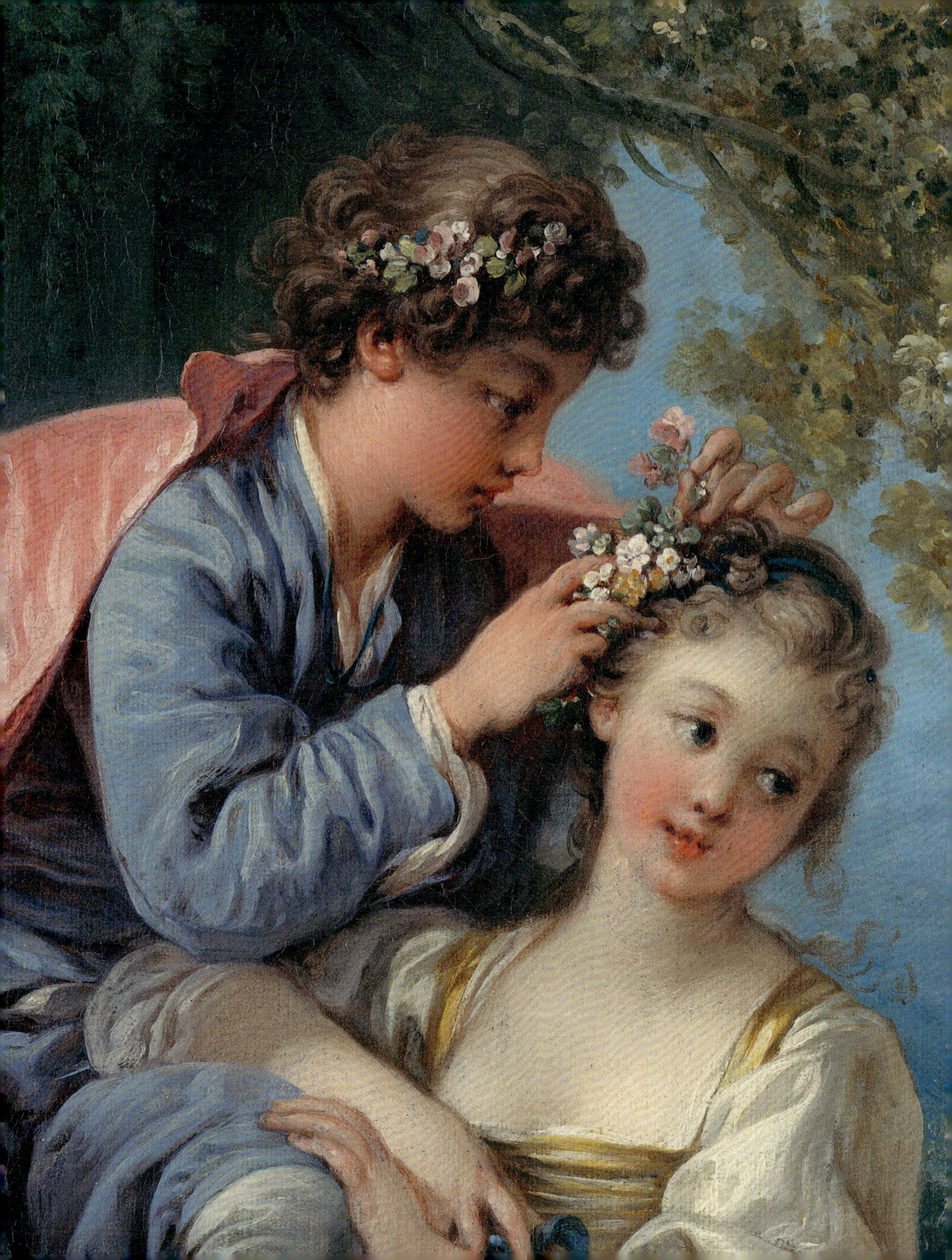

BOUCHER'S FOUR SEASONS

Xavier F. Salomon

Landscape-tones: steep skylines, low cloud, pearl ground with shadows in oyster and violet. Accidie. On the lake gunmetal and lemon. Summer: sand lilac sky. Autumn: swollen bruise greys. Winter: freezing white sand, clear skies, magnificent starscapes.

—Lawrence Durrell, *Justine*, 1957

In a letter of September 30, 1916, Virginia Bacon (1853–1919; fig. 1) wrote to Henry Clay Frick, "You may be surprised to receive this letter from me, after my declining to let you have the paintings of the 'Four Seasons' painted by Boucher by order of Louis XV for Madame de Pompadour."[1] "At the time I saw you," she continued, "I felt I could not part with them, as my brother-in-law was much attached to them, considering them to be the gems of his collection. . . . He would not part with them although he had many offers from Baron de Rothschild & others." The four paintings by François Boucher had appeared for sale in Paris on December 3, 1904, at the Galerie Georges Petit, where they were purchased by Eugène Fischhof (1853–1926), son-in-law of the celebrated art dealer Charles Sedelmeyer (1837–1925).[2] Fischhof, himself a dealer, promptly sold the paintings to the American railroad magnate and collector Edward Rathbone Bacon (1846–1915; fig. 2). At Bacon's death, in December 1915, his collection was inherited by his brother, Walter (1845–1917), and by his wife, Virginia (née Barker), a granddaughter of Cornelius Vanderbilt (1794–1877).[3] In Bacon's letter to Frick about the Boucher paintings, she concluded, "after much thought, I have made up my mind to part with them." On holiday at his summer home in Prides Crossing,

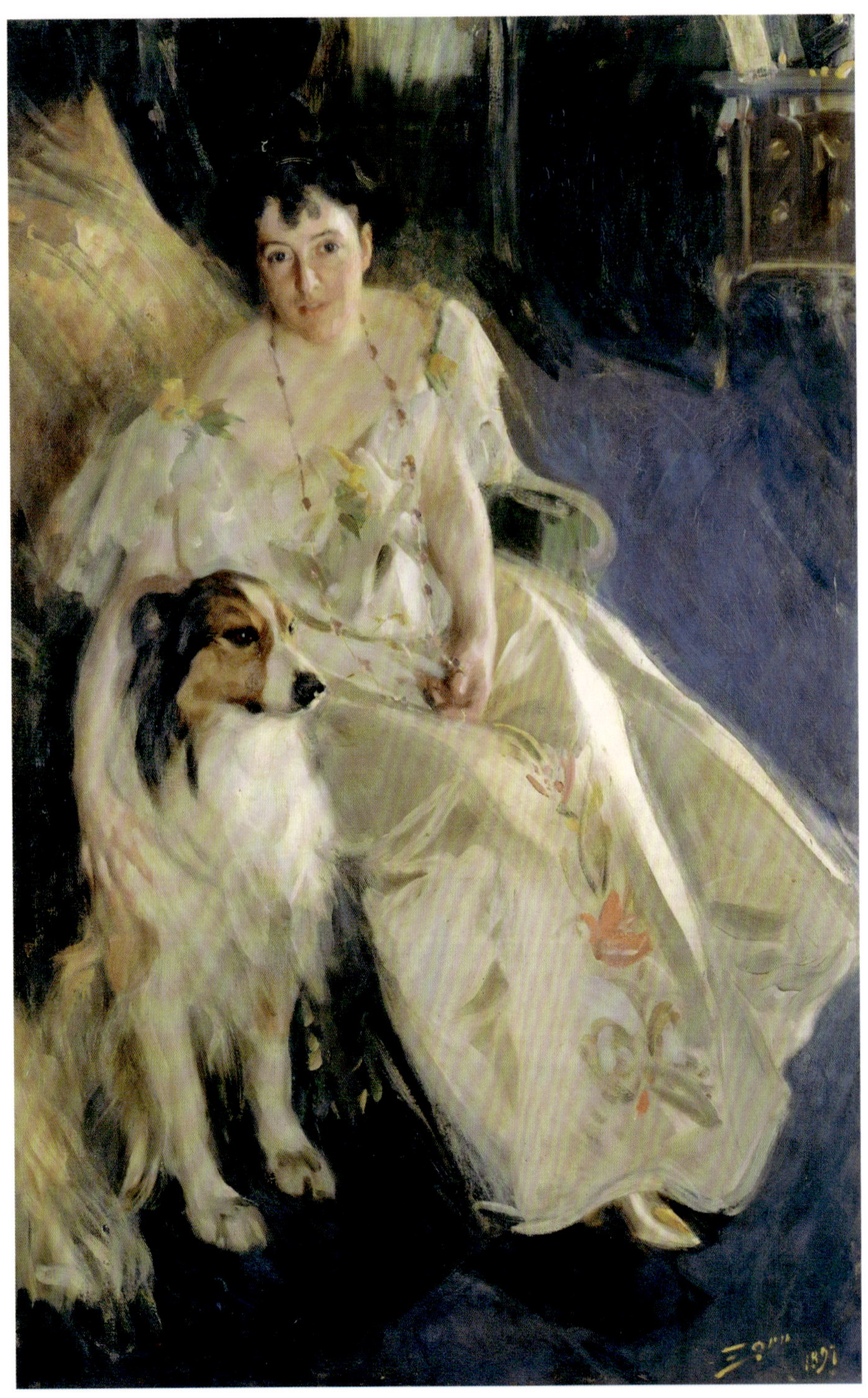

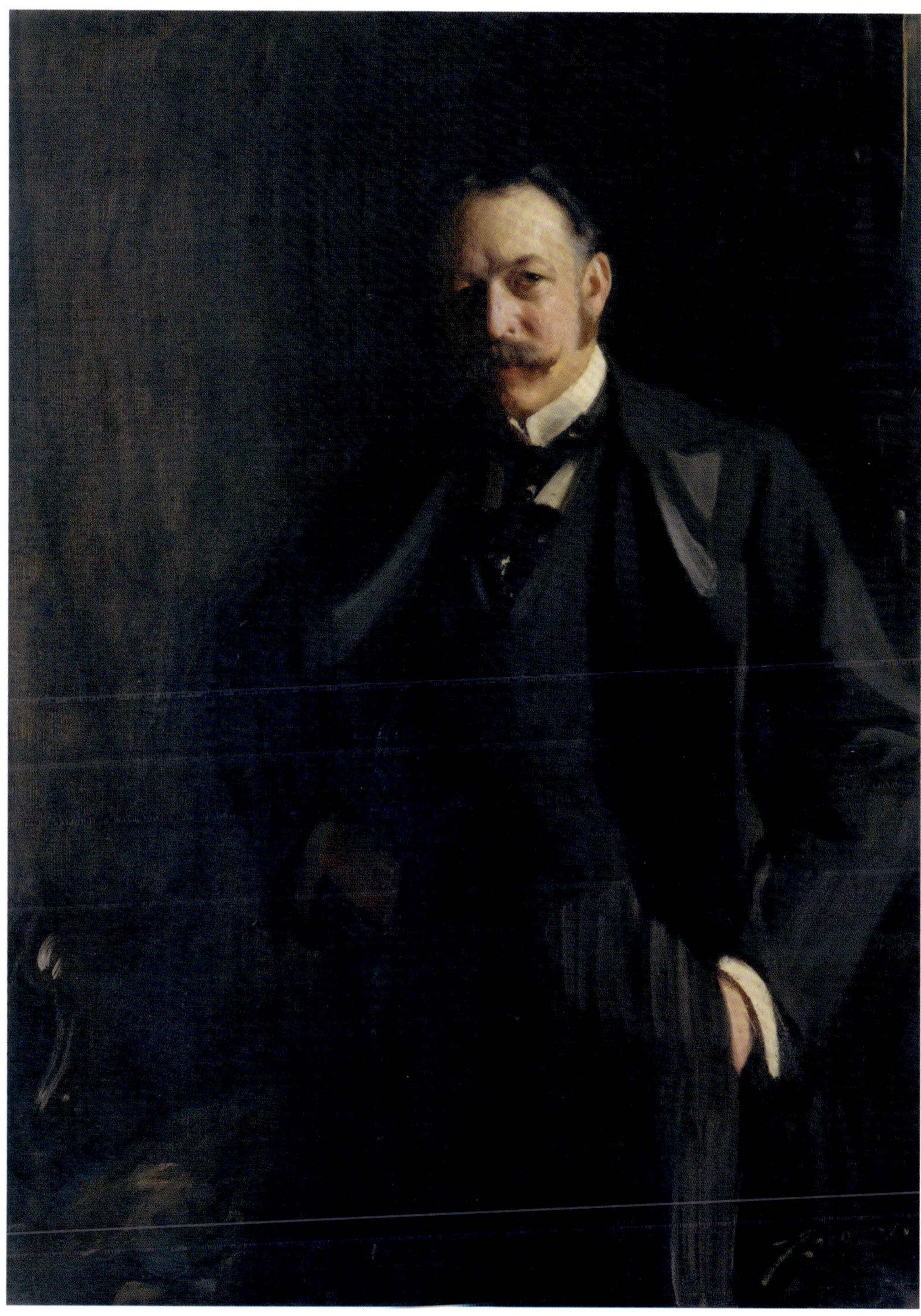

Massachusetts, at the time, Frick replied a few days later. On October 3, he wrote,

> Regarding your beautiful Bouchers, I never expected you would part with them, and I do not remember now what I said to you. Since our talk I have purchased eight very fine panels by Boucher, but owing to the association, I might still be willing to purchase yours, if you will kindly let me know what you think you should have for them. If I do not feel that I can pay the price, I can probably assist you in disposing of them.[4]

Just a few months before, in August 1916, Frick had acquired eight canvases representing the Arts and Sciences from the dealer Joseph Duveen (1869–1939) for $500,000.[5] These were believed to have been painted by Boucher for Madame de Pompadour's Château de Crécy. Frick bought the paintings for the boudoir of his wife, Adelaide—the so-called Boucher Room (fig. 3), on the second floor of the family's recently completed mansion at 1 East 70th Street in New York. Frick had a growing interest in French eighteenth-century painting.[6] The year before, in 1915, he had purchased *The Progress of Love*, a series of paintings by Jean-Honoré Fragonard (1732–1806). Boucher's *Four Seasons*, much smaller in size and scope than the two previously acquired cycles of canvases, appealed to Frick because of their quality, provenance, and importance in Edward Rathbone Bacon's collection. From her home at 247 Fifth Avenue, Virginia Bacon wrote back to Frick the next day, stating

Fig. 3
Boucher Room. The Frick
Collection, New York

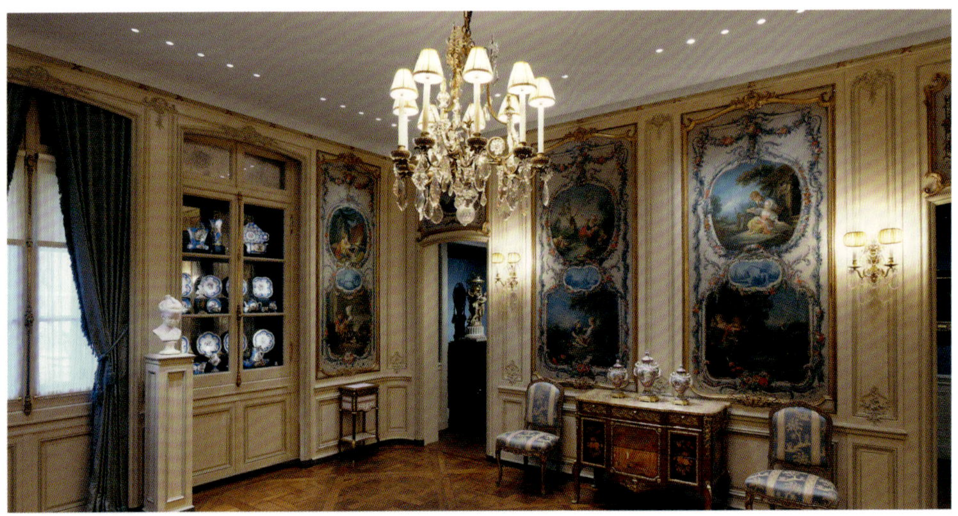

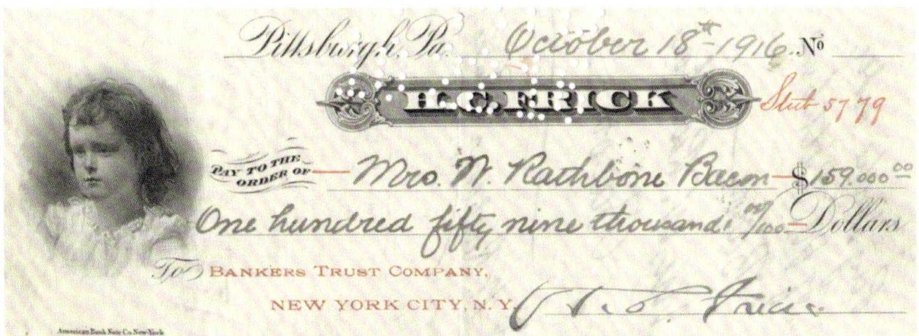

Fig. 4
Check of October 18, 1916, for the purchase of Boucher's *Four Seasons*. Art Collecting Files of Henry Clay Frick. The Frick Collection / Frick Art Research Library Archives

$159,000 as the asking price. On October 18, Frick sent Bacon a check for the full amount (fig. 4) accompanied by a note: "I hand you herewith [my] check for one hundred and fifty-nine thousand dollars, being the price you asked me for your four Bouchers. Please deliver them to the bearer." Frick then sent instructions to Thomas Kerr at Duveen Brothers: "Please go with your wagon to 247 Fifth Avenue this afternoon at four-thirty, and deliver the letter herewith to Mrs. Bacon. She will give you the four Bouchers I have purchased from her, which bring to my house and put in the gallery."[7]

On October 16, Frick cabled Duveen in Paris: "Have purchased four Bacon Bouchers. Will send size and original shape. Probably they are suitable for Boudoir."[8] Frick seems to have been considering including the four new canvases with the ensemble of eight paintings he had acquired in August. Duveen thought that only two of the *Seasons* should be included in the Boucher Room, with the other two displayed elsewhere in the house:

> So happy you secured Bouchers. They really finest existing nothin [*sic*] so fine by Boucher even in Louvre. Suggest hanging two opposite four hawthorn blue vases. Boucher Room well advanced. Will cable you tomorrow the two most suitable for room. I have photographs with rough sizes here . . . Compliments.[9]

In the end, none of the *Seasons* made it into Adelaide's boudoir. They were instead displayed in pairs facing each other in the passage leading from the entrance of the house to the garden overlooking Fifth Avenue—between the Dining Room and the Fragonard Room. By January 27, 1917, news of the purchase reached the *New York Times*. The article—titled "Frick Buys Four Bouchers"—reported that Frick was said "to have paid $200,000 for paintings representing Seasons."

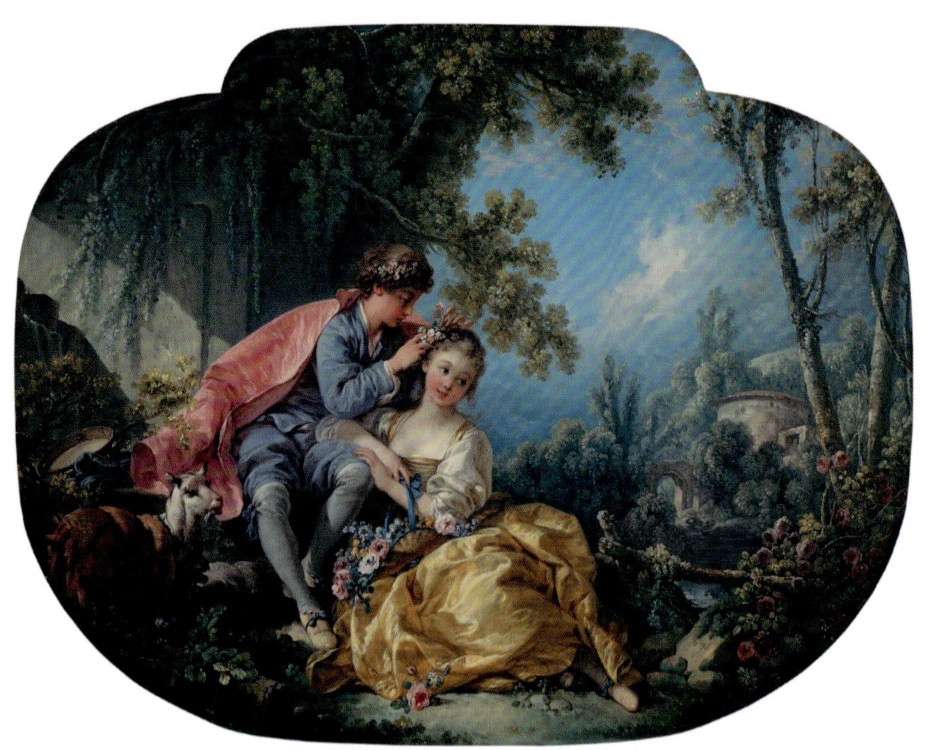

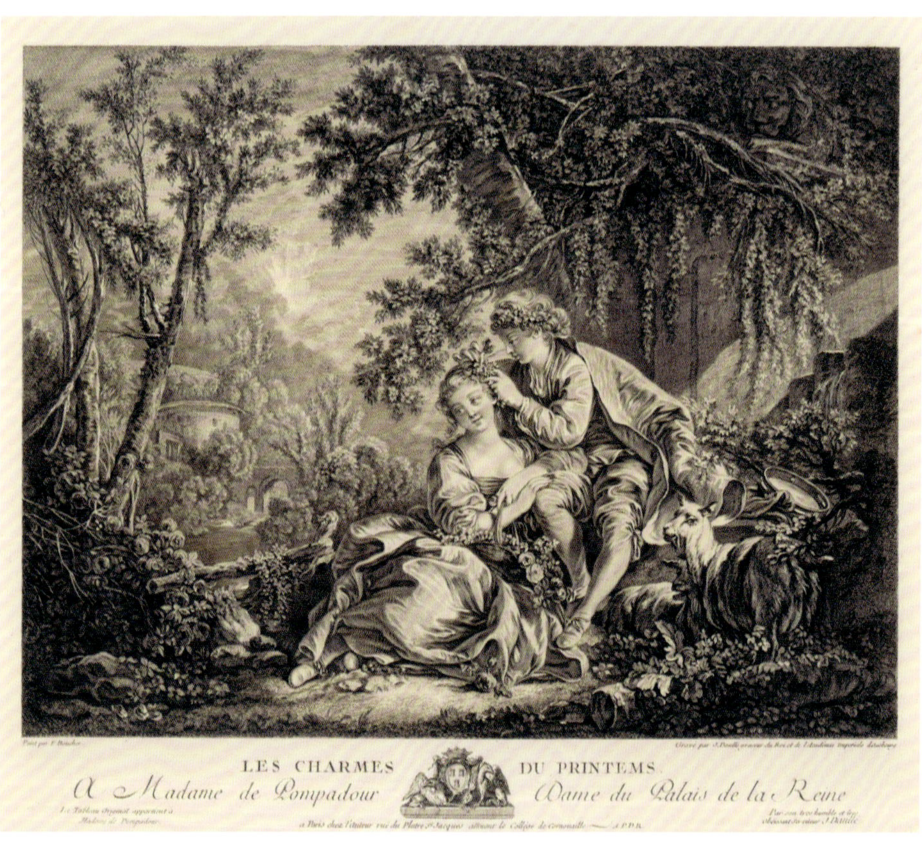

Peint par F. Boucher.
Gravé par J. Daullé graveur du Roi et de l'Académie impériale de Petersbourg.
LES CHARMES   DU PRINTEMS.
A Madame de Pompadour   Dame du Palais de la Reine.
Le Tableau Original appartient à
Madame de Pompadour.
Par son très humble et très
obéissant serviteur J. Daullé.
a Paris chez l'auteur rue du Platre St. Jacques attenant le Collège de Cornouaille.   A.P.D.R.

The Charms of Spring

A secluded glade, overgrown and sultry, opens up against a blue sky. On the left, a forbidding stone wall, covered in weeping foliage, is framed between a small, man-made waterfall and a tree growing diagonally out of the wall. The plants' foliage ranges in tone from bluish green to warmer, yellower shades. Opposite the wall is a pair of slender trees, closing the scene to the right. In between, a landscape view opens toward the far distance. It is a narrow valley, below a shallow hill, both covered in vegetation and by the side of a body of water: a river or, more likely, a small lake. In the foreground on the right, a cluster of pink roses grows wildly below the trees and climbs over a group of small rocks. Behind the trees on the right is a round stone building with a tiled roof that is blocked in by two arches. There is a sense of the building being somewhat neglected. This is Boucher's setting for the first painting of *The Four Seasons* that Frick had purchased: *Spring* (fig. 5).[10]

The focus of the painting is the couple in the foreground. At the center of the painting is a young woman with blond hair, fair skin, and rosy lips. She wears a voluminous yellow dress over a simple white shirt. Her white shoes with blue ribbons peak out from beneath her gown. Her lower arms and décolletage are bare. With her left arm, she holds a straw basket—possibly a hat—lined with a blue ribbon, in which she has placed cut roses (pink and white) and other small wildflowers (white, yellow, blue, and lilac). Her right arm and left hand rest sensuously over the left leg of the young man seated next to her. He is dressed in blue with a billowing pink cloak and white stockings. With a tambourine at his side, he seems to have just stopped making music. Small pink flowers—presumably just placed there by the young woman—decorate his flowing, brown hair. He is captured at the moment of reciprocating the action: he tenderly places a bunch of tiny white and pink flowers in her hair, mirroring his own coiffure. Looking toward the young woman, the man is blushing. She looks away to the far distance, but her hand, gently placed on the man's knee, indicates their loving relationship. With the arrival of spring, we are witnessing the tender blossoming of love among the flowers of this charmed clearing.

While based somewhat on contemporary fashion, the couple's clothing is of a type associated, in eighteenth-century France, with shepherds and shepherdesses in a mythical, Arcadian countryside, a pastoral theme that often appeared in Boucher's work and that of his contemporaries. To reinforce the

Fig. 5
François Boucher
The Four Seasons: Spring, 1755
Oil on canvas
21⅜ × 28⅝ in. (54.3 × 72.7 cm)
The Frick Collection, New York

Fig. 6
Jean Daullé, after François Boucher
Les Charmes du printems (The Charms of Spring), 1756
Etching on paper
12¹⁵⁄₁₆ × 16¹⁵⁄₁₆ in. (329 × 430 mm)
Musée du Louvre, Département des Arts Graphiques, Paris

pastoral subject, two goats are placed next to the young man, suggesting that this amatory moment represents an interruption of his duties as a shepherd.

Between 1748 and 1761, the printmaker Jean Daullé (1703–1763) produced a number of etchings based on paintings by Boucher; and, around 1756, he printed copies of the artist's *Four Seasons*.[11] Each print was accompanied by a title that identifies the season depicted. *Spring* is captioned *Les Charmes du printems* (The Charms of Spring) (fig. 6).

The Pleasures of Summer

As the seasons shift from spring into summer, so does the mood of Boucher's paintings. From the fresh valley inhabited by shepherd and shepherdess, we move farther into the woods for summer, the breezes of spring giving way to sultry heat. Like *Spring, Summer* (fig. 7) is divided in two halves: the dense woodland on the right and the more open wilderness to the left. A body of water is, again, visible at the bottom left, leaving the impression that we are at a location along the lake, not far from where the previous scene was set. But we are removed from the human realm, in a more fabulous location. At the center of the canvas, a fountain stands among the trees. The fountain is decorated with stone sculptures of two putti frolicking on the back of a dolphin, from whose mouth water spouts and descends into the basin below.

Along the banks of the lake, three women are taking advantage of the fresh water. The one on the right, sitting under the trees, has discarded her voluminous clothes: draperies in rich orange, yellow, and silver and lilac fabrics that rest in a pile by the side. As she removes her white shirt, her legs and left shoulder are exposed. Her hair is elegantly coiffed, with a blue ribbon, identifying her as an aristocrat. Resting against their clothes, her two companions are nude, their pink flesh set against clouds of pink, white, and green textiles. They sport similar hairdos, with red ribbons. The woman on the left is partly in the lake, while the middle one is dipping her left leg into the water.

The central figure in the painting is seen from the back, with her shoulders and sinuous body lying over the fabric, exposing her bottom to the viewer. The woman on the left is partly concealed by the rushes on the side of the lake, while the third one is undressing. Vaguely looking at each other, they seem oblivious to any chance viewers. Boucher puts the viewer in a voyeuristic position at this moment of female intimacy, as if stumbling upon a secret scene. The sweetness of the pastoral figures in *Spring* here gives way to a sensual atmosphere. While the fountain is very much in the spirit of paintings by Boucher, Fragonard, and Jean-Antoine Watteau (1684–1721) and typical of eighteenth-century French paintings, the presentation of the three female figures is in a long tradition of Western art. In antiquity, Roman painters represented the graceful forms of nude females lying down. In the Renaissance, especially in the work of Titian (ca. 1488–1576), nude goddesses and nymphs became part of the iconographical repertoire of painters. In *Summer*, it is

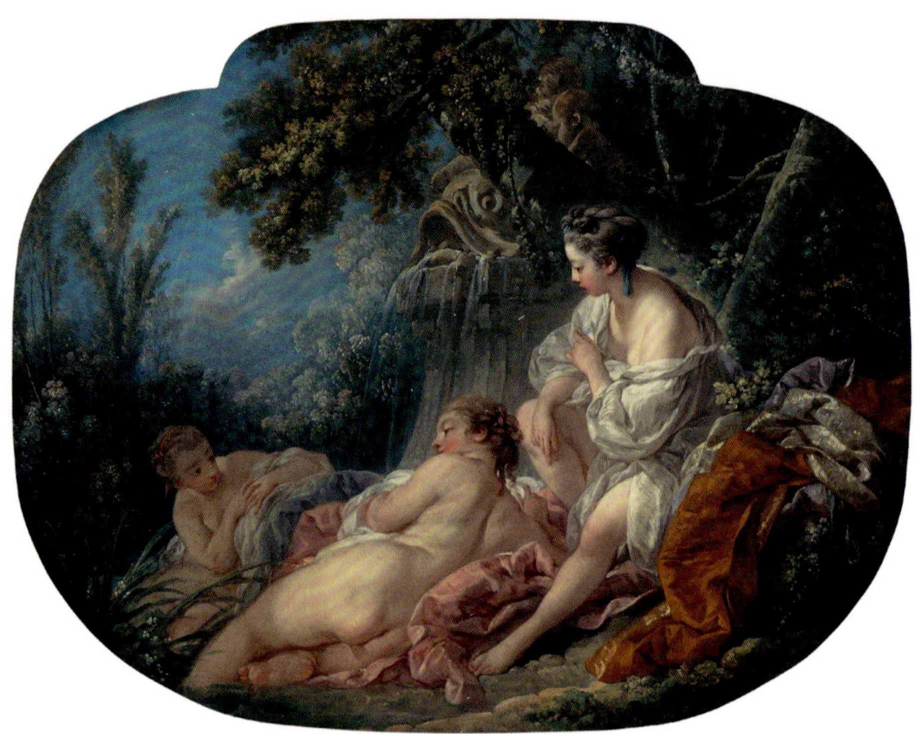

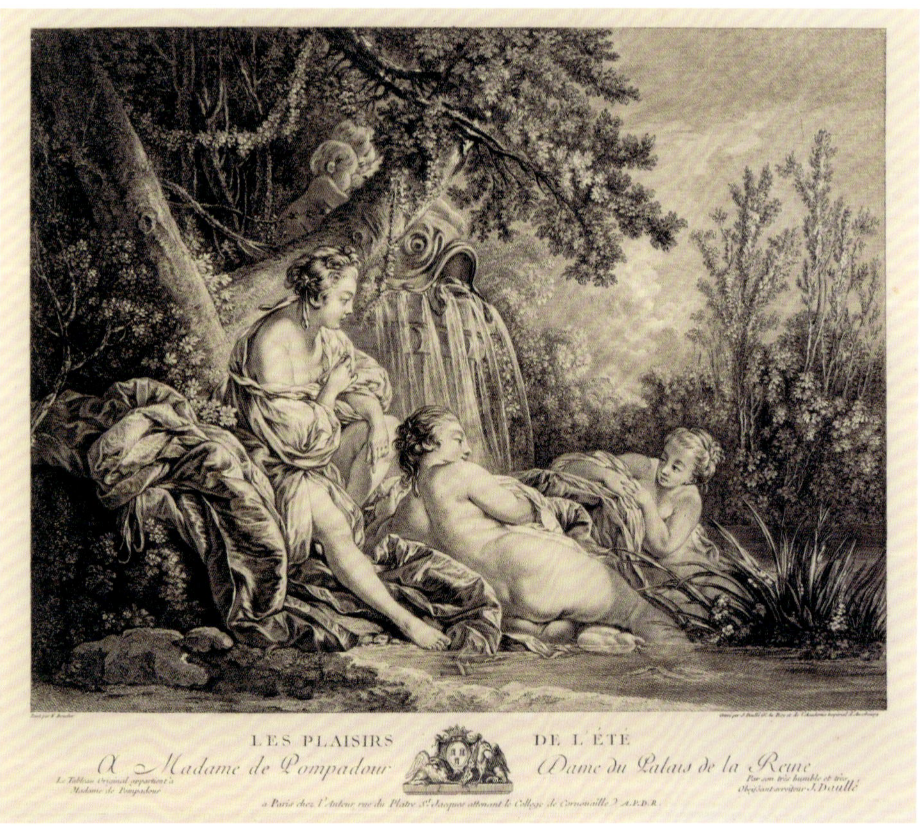

Peint par F. Boucher
Gravé par J. Daullé Gr. du Roi et de l'Académie Imperial d'Augsbourg
LES PLAISIRS   DE L'ÉTÉ
A Madame de Pompadour   Dame du Palais de la Reine
Le Tableau Original appartient à
Madame de Pompadour
Par son très humble et très
Obeïssant serviteur J. Daullé
à Paris chez l'Auteur, rue du Platre St. Jacques attenant le College de Cornoüaille ? A.P.D.R.

unclear if we are seeing a group of ladies-in-waiting or noblewomen taking a break in the woods of Versailles or, instead, a group of mythical goddesses, naiads, or nymphs. Daullé's print (fig. 8) after Boucher's *Summer* is titled *Les Plaisirs de l'été* (The Pleasures of Summer), alluding not only to the pleasures of the season but also to those of the flesh.

Fig. 7
François Boucher
The Four Seasons: Summer, 1755
Oil on canvas
22½ × 28⅝ in. (57.2 × 72.7 cm)
The Frick Collection, New York

Fig. 8
Jean Daullé, after François
Boucher
Les Plaisirs de l'été (The Pleasures
of Summer), 1756
Etching on paper
13⅛ × 16¹⁵⁄₁₆ in. (333 × 430 mm)
Musée du Louvre, Département
des Arts Graphiques, Paris

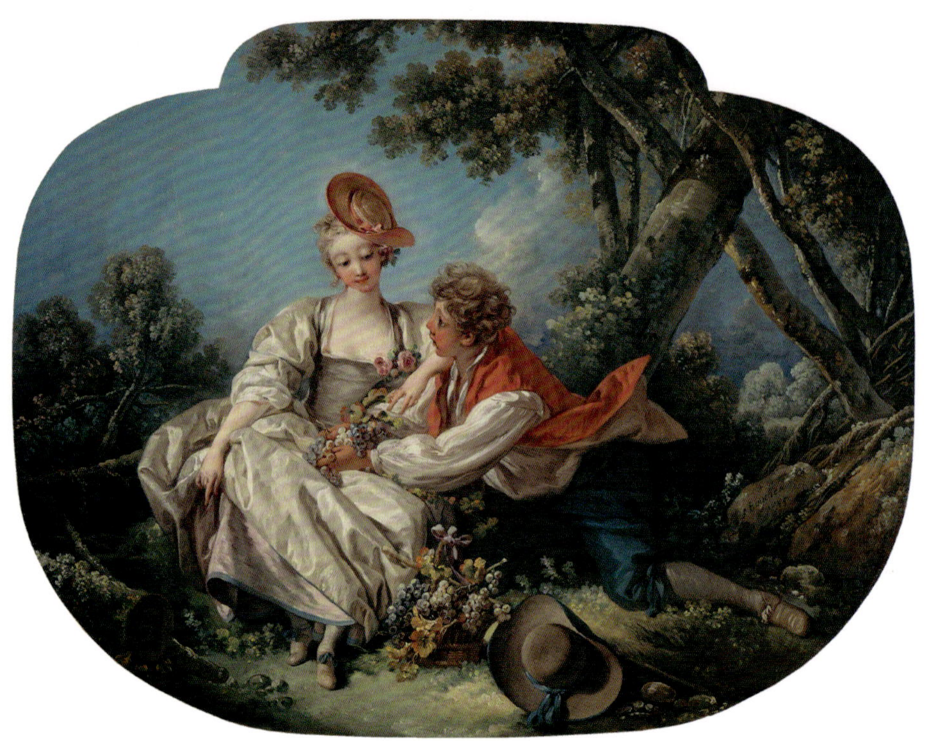

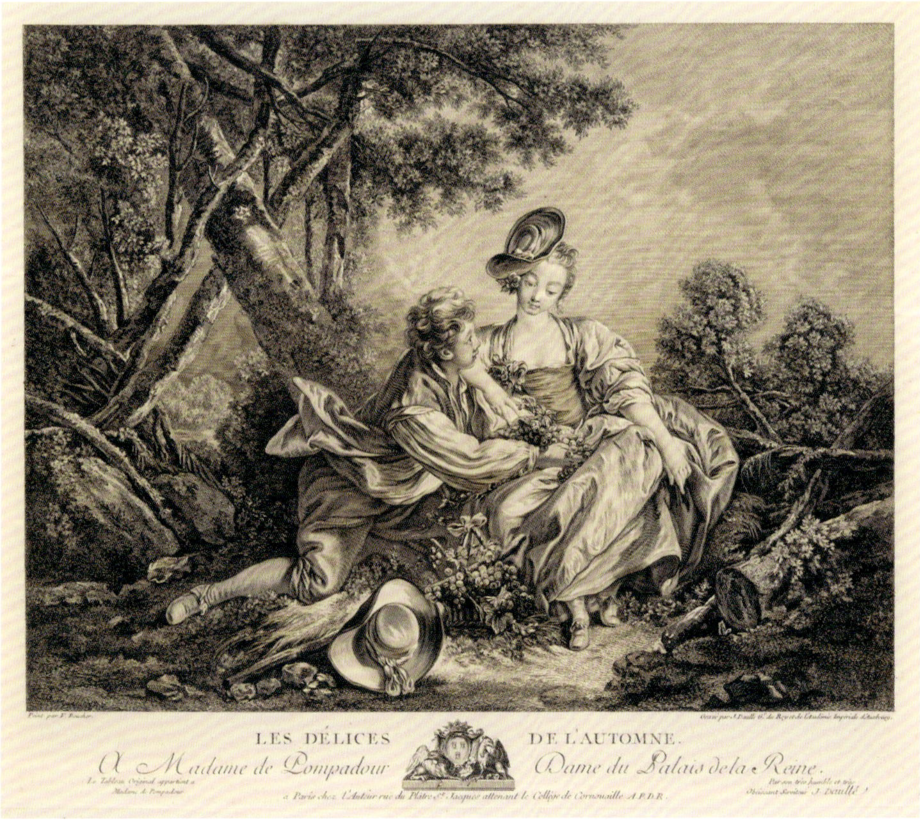

Peint par F. Boucher.
Gravé par J. Daullé gr. du Roy et de l'Académie Impériale de Petersbourg.
LES DÉLICES
DE L'AUTOMNE.
A Madame de Pompadour
Dame du Palais de la Reine.
Le Tableau Original appartient a
Madame de Pompadour
a Paris chez l'Auteur rue du Platre St. Jacques attenant le Collège de Cornouaille A.P.D.R.
Par son très humble et très
Obéissant Serviteur J. Daullé

The Joys of Autumn

With *Autumn* (fig. 9), we are back in the pastoral land of Arcadia. Again, we are in the woods, away from human dwellings. Trees to the right grow in a lush meadow, with a background of more trees to the left. A young woman and man, dressed like the couple in *Spring*, are in the foreground. The man wears bright blue breeches and white stockings, a white shirt, and a red vest. The woman, seated at the center of the composition, is in a white dress trimmed in light blue with roses in her décolletage. A straw hat—probably the same type shown in *Spring*—is coquettishly placed on her head. The man's felt hat and his shepherd's staff are on the ground, in front of her. Were it not for the absence of flowers, the scene could as well be set in a similar landscape and time as *Spring*. However, a wicker basket, at center bottom of the painting, is filled with white and red grapes, identifying the season as autumn. While the shepherdess sits splendidly under the trees, the young man flings himself at her feet, placing more grapes in her lap. In this courtly, pastoral scene, the love between the two figures is clearly displayed. Daullé, once again, expanded on the title of this season: *Les Délices de l'automne* (The Joys of Autumn) (fig. 10).

Fig. 9
François Boucher
The Four Seasons: Autumn, 1755
Oil on canvas
22¼ × 28¼ in. (56.5 × 73 cm)
The Frick Collection, New York

Fig. 10
Jean Daullé, after François Boucher
Les Délices de l'automne (The Joys of Autumn), 1756
Etching on paper
12¹⁵⁄₁₆ × 17 in. (329 × 431 mm)
Musée du Louvre, Département des Arts Graphiques, Paris

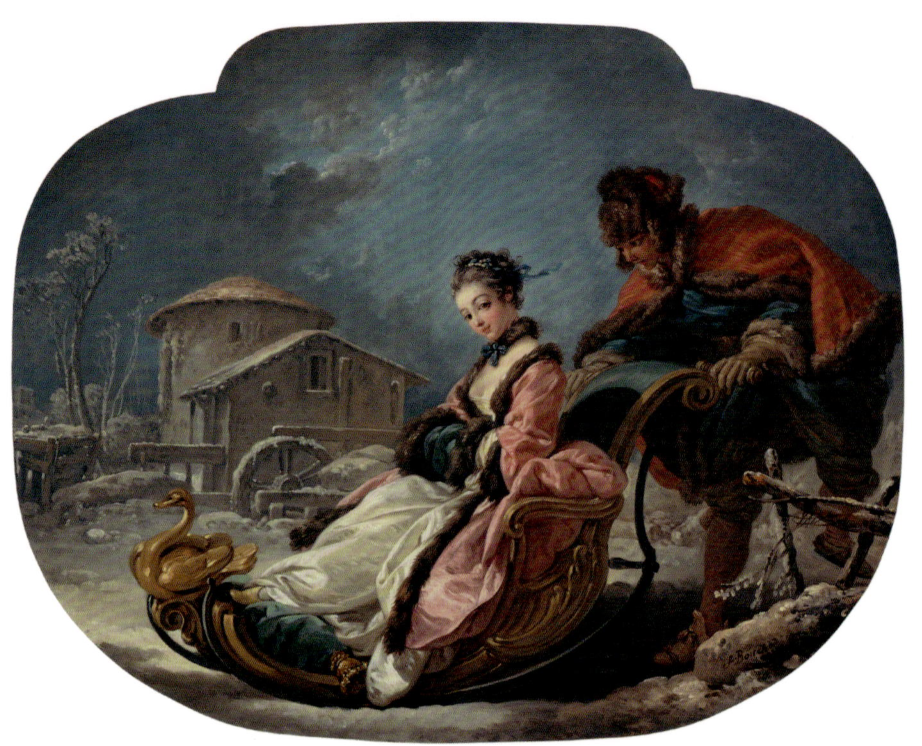

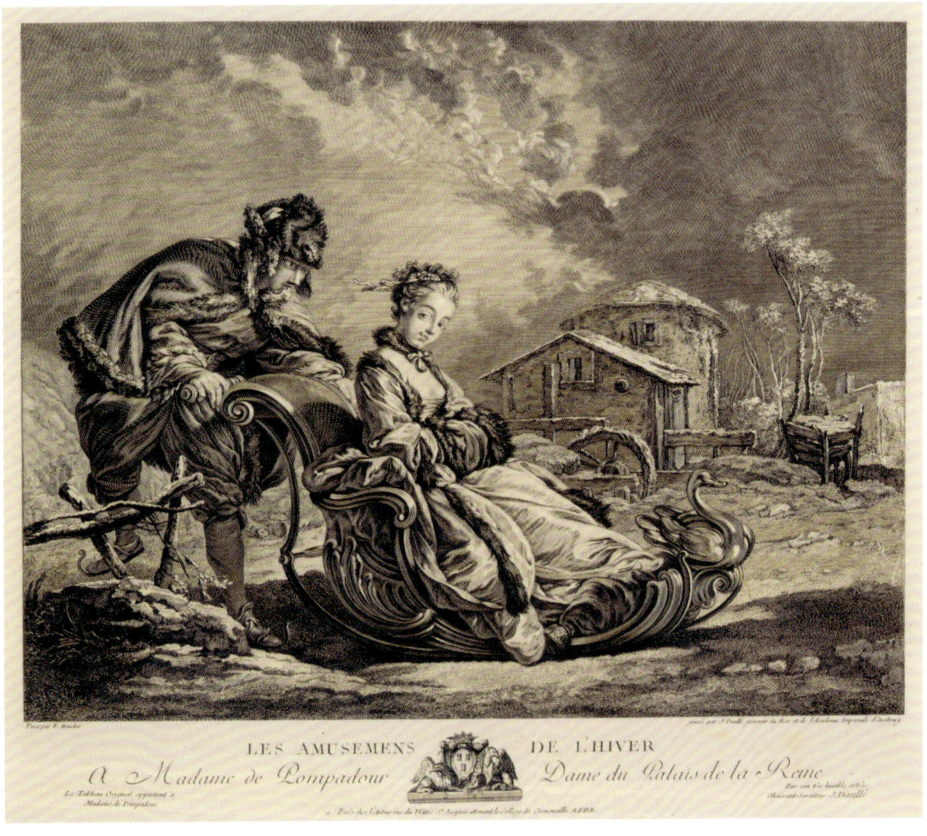

Peint par F. Boucher
gravé par J. Daullé, graveur du Roi et de l'Academie Imperiale d'Ausbourg
LES AMUSEMENS DE L'HIVER
A Madame de Pompadour Dame du Palais de la Reine
Le Tableau Original appartient à Madame de Pompadour
Par son très humble, et très obeissant Serviteur J. Daullé
a Paris chez l'Auteur rue du Platre St Jacques attenant le College de Grenoville A.P.D.R.

The Amusements of Winter

In *Winter* (fig. 11), we are out of the woods. Next to a few frozen and barren trees is a circular stone building—similar in shape to the one in the background of *Spring*—with a wheel attached to it. Another body of water is indicated by the frozen wheel of the mill and the icy expanse—presumably a frozen lake or pond—on which the young man is skating and pushing the elaborate gilt-metal sleigh in which the young woman is seated. The sky is blue, but dark clouds gather on the left, behind the trees and the mill. Upholstered in green velvet, the back of the sleigh is like an armchair, while the front has a decorative finial in the shape of a swan. A large cushion, also in green velvet, with a large, gilded tassel, is at the foot of the woman, who wears an elegant white dress, a pink, fur-lined cloak, and yellow slippers. Her hair is styled in a manner similar to that of the ladies in *Summer*, with a blue ribbon accompanied by pearls. The ribbon flutters in the wind as she is pushed across the ice. Although the woman's cloak and fur-lined muff are meant to keep her warm, her décolletage is exposed and her neck is barely covered. She is clearly on display, in her elaborate sleigh. Incidentally, of the nine figures that populate Boucher's *Four Seasons*, she is the only one who looks straight out at the viewer.

The man pushing the sleigh wears green breeches, a blue fur-lined jacket, a red fur-lined cloak, rust-colored stockings, a big fur hat, and gloves. Is he a lover or a servant (or both)? Eighteenth-century sources describe the figure as a "Tatar," pointing out that the man's costume is surely influenced by typical northern clothing from Central Asia, Poland, or Russia.[12] Daullé's print after the painting bears the title *Les Amusemens de l'hiver* (The Amusements of Winter) (fig. 12).

Fig. 11
François Boucher
The Four Seasons: Winter, 1755
Oil on canvas
22⅜ × 28¾ in. (56.8 × 73 cm)
The Frick Collection, New York

Fig. 12
Jean Daullé, after François Boucher
Les Amusemens de l'hiver (The Amusements of Winter), 1756
Etching on paper
13 × 17 1/16 in. (330 × 433 mm)
Musée du Louvre, Département des Arts Graphiques, Paris

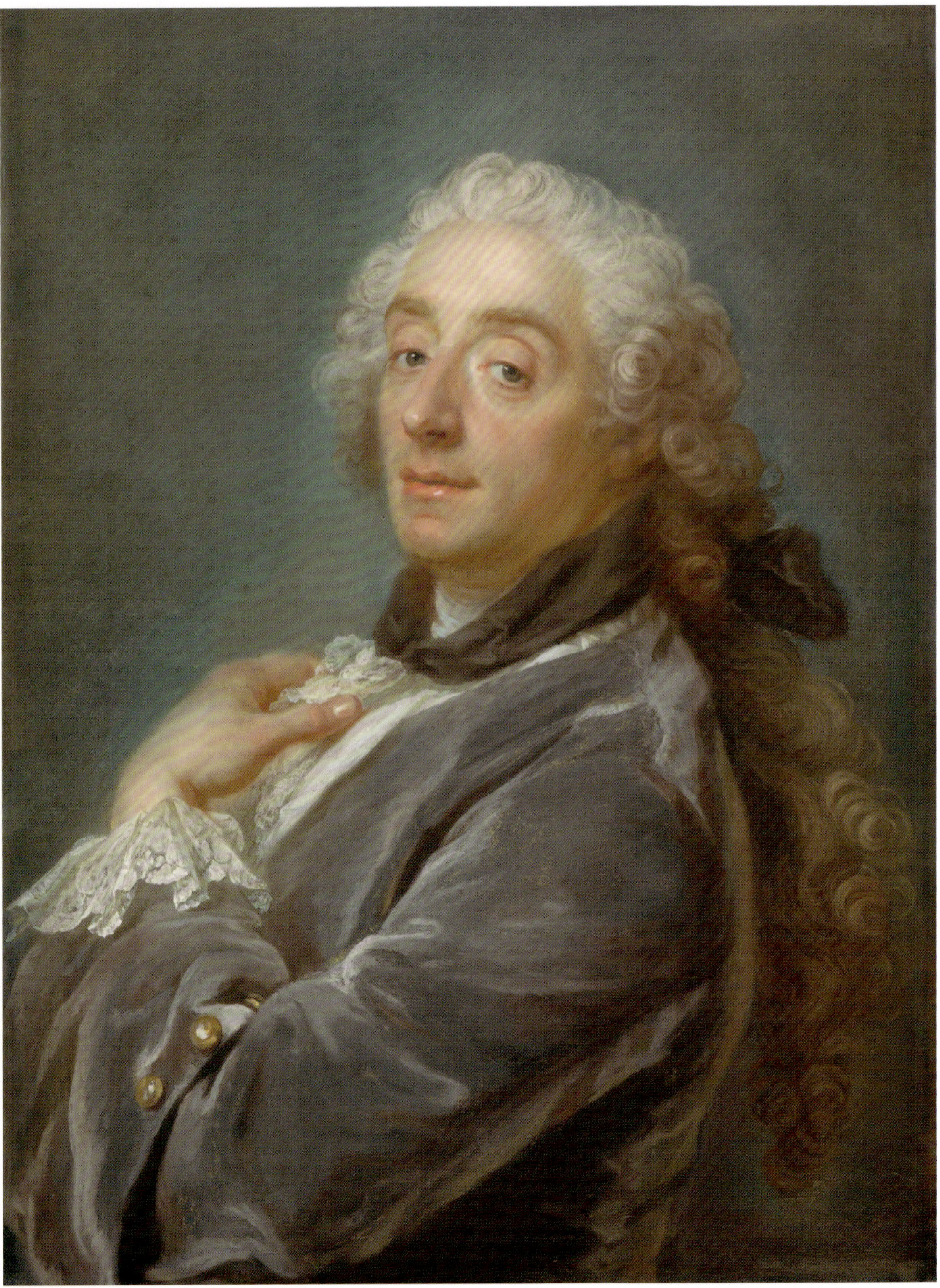

The Artist: François Boucher

Boucher was born in Paris on September 29, 1703, and died there on May 30, 1770 (fig. 13).[13] Apart from about three years in Italy, his five-decade-long career was spent in the French capital. Three of the paintings in *The Four Seasons* series are signed and dated 1755, by which time the painter was fifty-two years old and at the height of his career (fig. 14). His progress as an artist, however, had not been easy. His father, Nicolas (ca. 1672–1743), was a mediocre Parisian painter, connected to the Académie de Saint-Luc (Academy of St. Luke), a far less prestigious school than that of the Académie Royale de Peinture et de Sculpture (Royal Academy of Painting and Sculpture). Young François most likely learned to paint from his father but, as a young man, was taken under the wing of the far more talented François Lemoyne (1688–1737). In 1723, he won the Prix de Rome but due to financial constraints was unable to travel to Rome. Instead, in the 1720s, he established a fruitful partnership with the publisher Jean-François Cars (1661–1730), for whom he provided designs for prints. For about a decade, while still painting, Boucher worked mainly for the print market, producing etchings after Watteau's works for Jean de Jullienne (1686–1766) and illustrating books. In the spring of 1728, he was finally able to travel to Rome, where he was based at the Académie de France until 1731, when he returned to Paris. While in Italy, Boucher

Fig. 13
Gustav Lundberg
François Boucher, 1741
Pastel on paper
25 ⅝ × 19 ¾ in. (65 × 50 cm)
Musée du Louvre, Paris

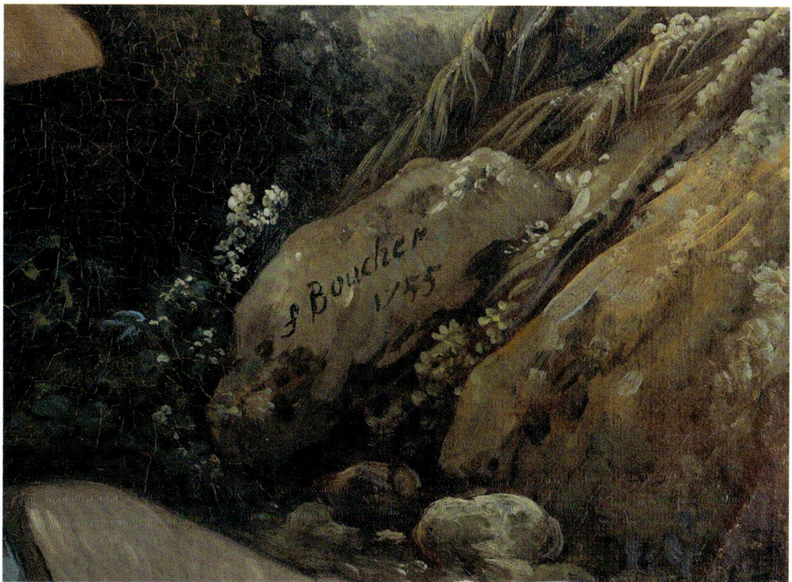

Fig. 14
Detail of the signature from François Boucher, *The Four Seasons: Autumn*, 1755 (fig. 9)

Fig. 15
François Boucher
Hercules and Omphale, ca. 1730
Oil on canvas
35 7/16 × 29 1/8 in. (90 × 74 cm)
Pushkin State Museum of Fine
Arts, Moscow

Following pages:

Fig. 16
François Boucher
The Crocodile Hunt, 1739
Oil on canvas
72 7/16 × 50 9/16 in.
(184 × 128.5 cm)
Musée de Picardie, Amiens

Fig. 17
François Boucher
Le Pasteur galant (The Gallant
Shepherd), 1733–39
Oil on canvas
58 × 78 in. (147 × 198 cm)
Archives Nationales, Hôtel de
Subise, Paris

Fig. 18
François Boucher
Le Pasteur complaisant (The Kind
Shepherd), 1733–39
Oil on canvas
56 × 74 1/2 in. (142 × 189 cm)
Archives Nationales, Hôtel de
Subise, Paris

absorbed important lessons from studying the paintings of local baroque artists. His *Hercules and Omphale* (fig. 15), painted in the early 1730s (while in Rome or soon after his return to Paris) encapsulates the artistic achievements of the young painter: erotic mythological scenes that would have appealed to a French audience.

Upon his return to France, Boucher was approved (*agréé*) at the Académie Royale in November 1731 and received (*reçu*) into the esteemed institution in January 1734. In the 1730s, he established himself as a painter of mythological subjects for a range of patrons. In 1735, he received his first royal commission— for four paintings of putti for the *chambre de la reine* (queen's bedroom) at Versailles. Soon after, between 1736 and 1738, he was asked to produce two canvases for the dining room of the king's *petits appartements* (private apartments), also at Versailles. The two canvases—*The Leopard Hunt* and *The Crocodile Hunt* (fig. 16)—were part of a series of eight paintings (nine were produced, but one was replaced) with work by the most prominent artists of the time: Jean-François de Troy (1679–1752), Charles Parrocel (1688–1752), Nicolas Lancret (1690–1743), Jean-Baptiste Pater (1695–1736), and Carle Van Loo (1705–1765).[14] While working for the king, Boucher painted some religious works and continued to work for the print market—both creating prints and having his paintings engraved by others—but he also began to be known for a genre that would become associated with his name: pastoral imagery with amorous shepherds and shepherdesses. (These were often inspired by contemporary theater and ballet, a world in which Boucher was directly involved.) In 1738–39, for example, he painted two overdoors for the Hôtel de Soubise in Paris—*Le Pasteur galant* (The Gallant Shepherd) (fig. 17) and *Le Pasteur complaisant* (The Kind Shepherd) (fig. 18)—which are forerunners of the Frick's *Four Seasons* in both subject matter and style.

Boucher's work became even more sought after in the 1740s and 1750s. He worked on a regular basis for the king, creating works for the royal residences of Versailles, Fontainebleau, Choisy, and Marly, among others. He became particularly popular for his erotic subjects, such as the celebrated *Odalisque brune* (The Dark-Haired Odalisque) (fig. 19).[15] The unknown model in the painting is resting provocatively on a Turkish-style divan covered in sheets and cushions, next to a small table with mounted porcelain and jewels. This type of Boucher painting—which was based on mythological depictions of Venus and Diana in Italian paintings from the sixteenth and seventeenth centuries—

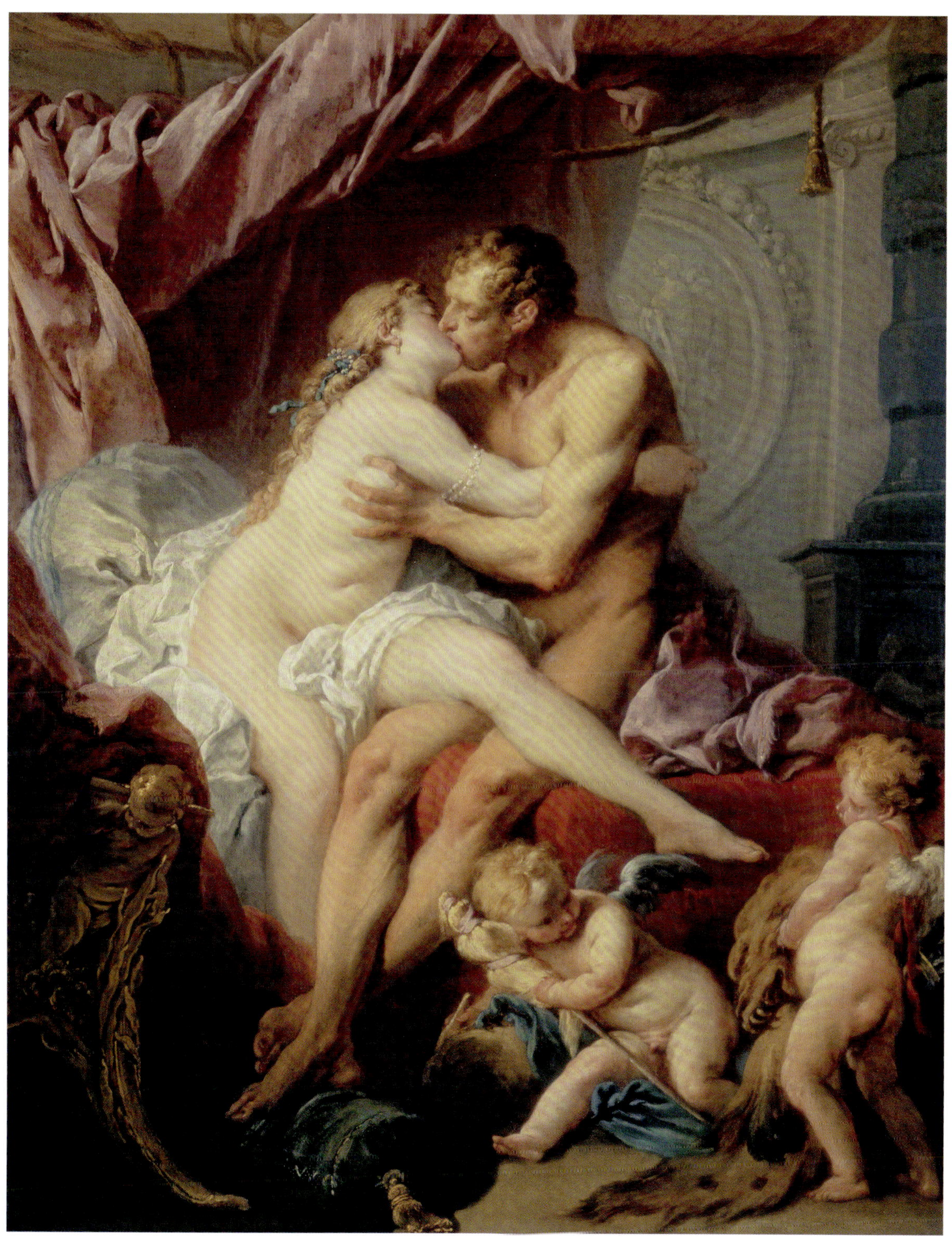

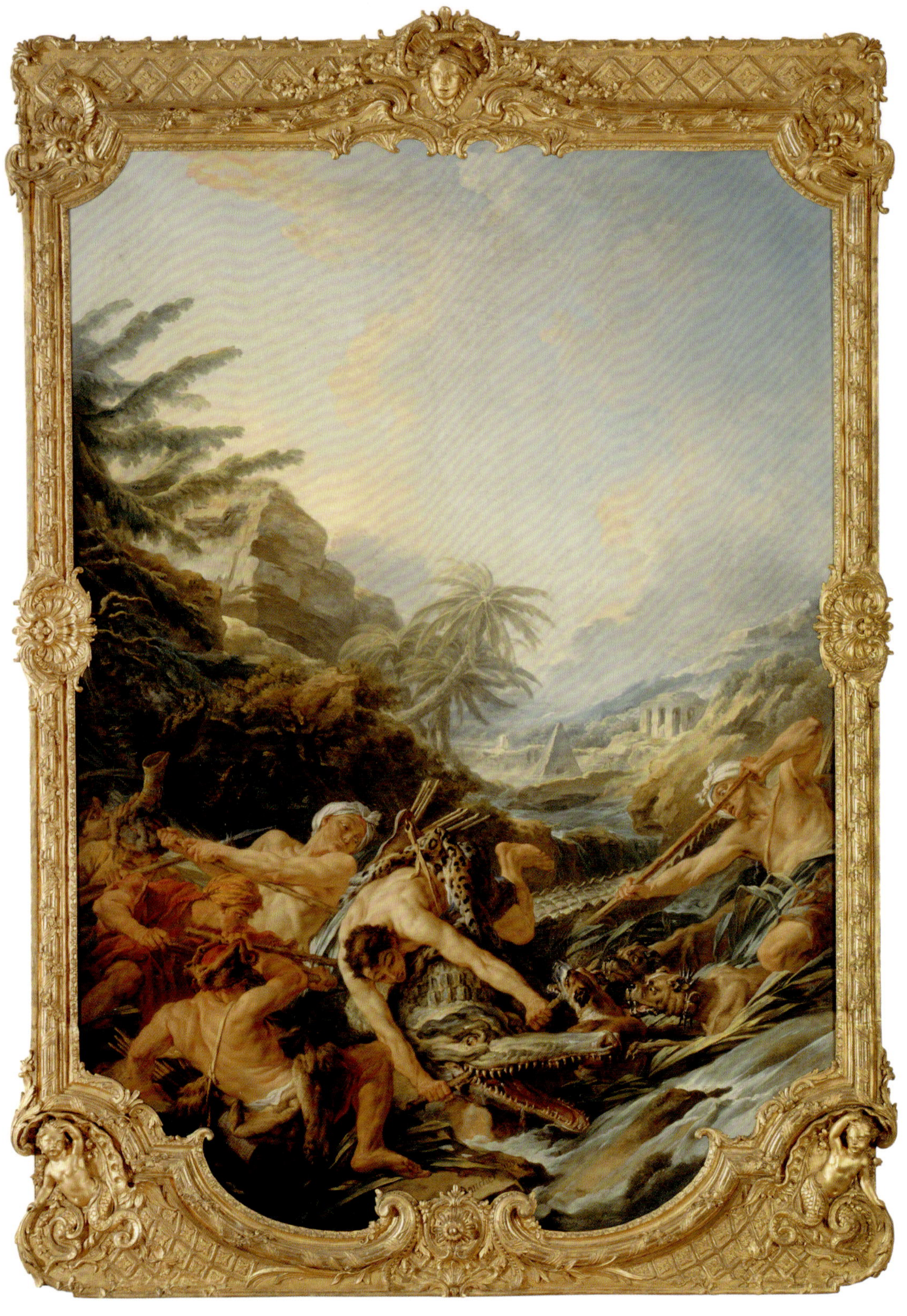

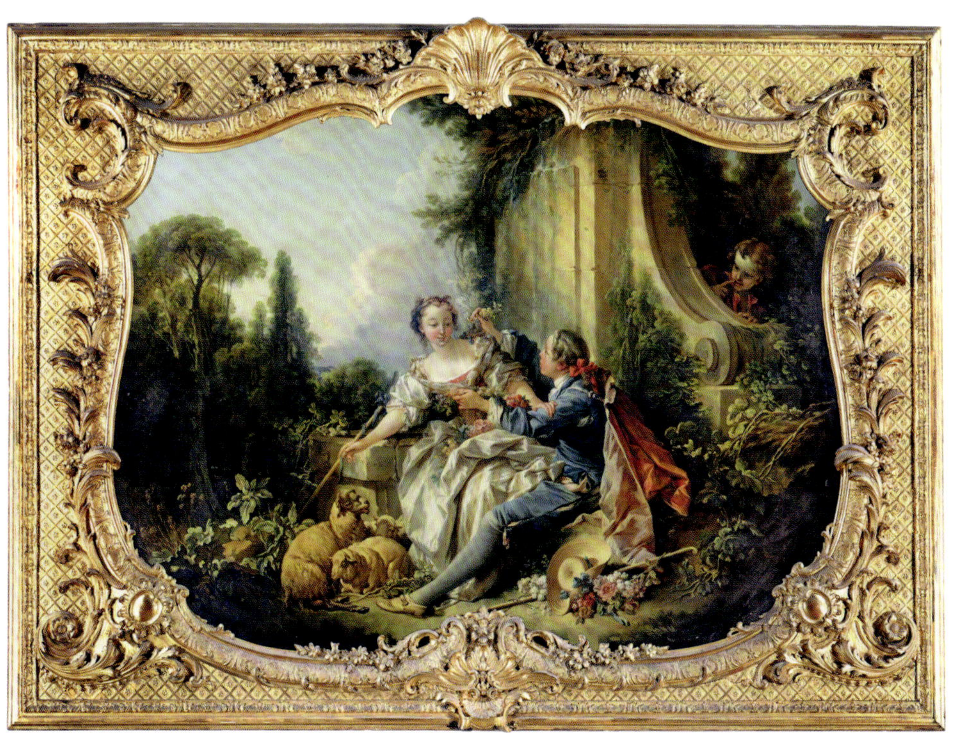

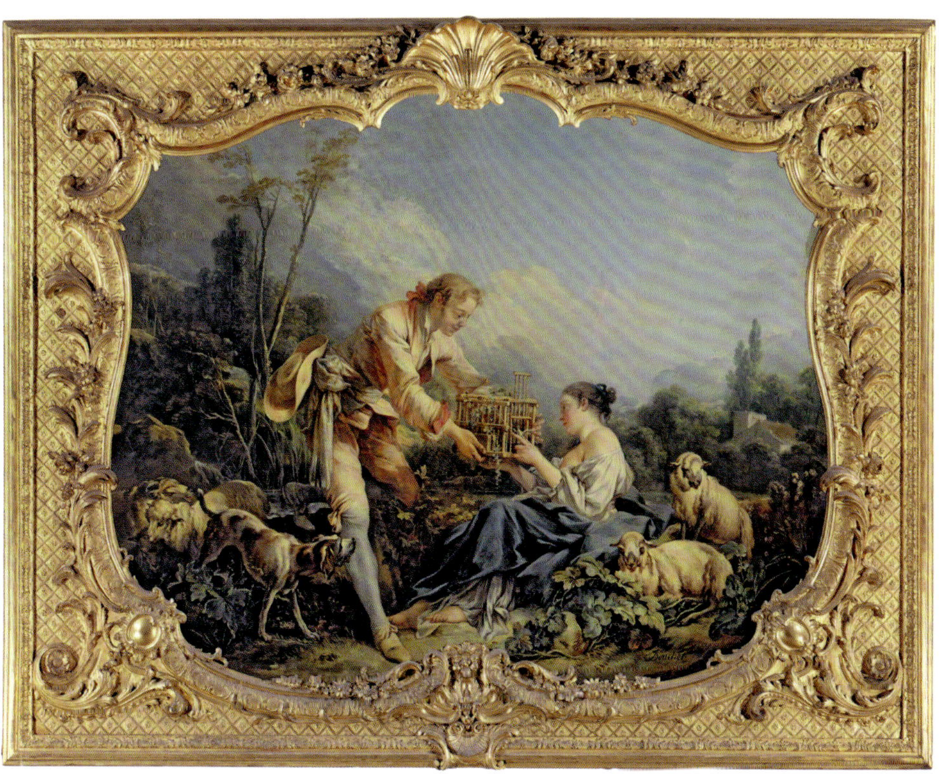

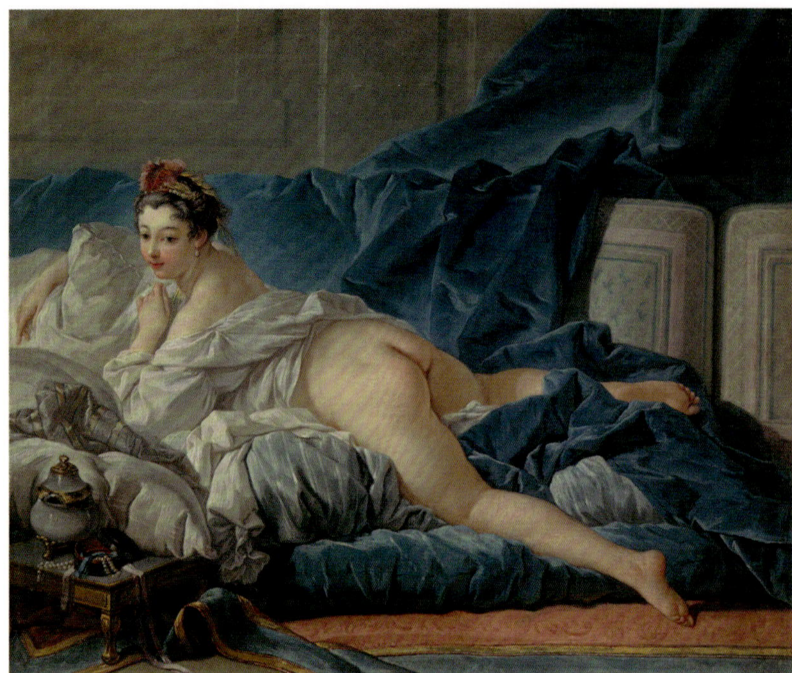

Fig. 19
François Boucher
L'Odalisque brune (The Dark-Haired Odalisque), 1745
Oil on canvas
21 × 25½ in. (53.5 × 64.5 cm)
Musée du Louvre, Paris

would have attracted the patronage of men from the royal court and the *haute bourgeoisie* of Paris. Moreover, a painting such as *L'Odalisque brune* would have been the archetype for works such as *Summer* from *The Four Seasons*.

In the mid-1730s, Boucher started to produce designs and cartoons for tapestries. He had already worked for the print market and also began to promote his compositions through the porcelain manufactories of Vincennes and Sèvres.[16] The artist first provided models for the Beauvais tapestry factory, producing many celebrated designs that were replicated throughout the eighteenth century and assured his wide fame.[17] In 1755, Boucher was appointed *inspecteur sur les ouvrages* (controller of tapestry production) at the rival Gobelins factory. Through prints after his paintings and tapestry designs, his work began to be replicated, not only on porcelain pieces but also on textiles and furniture, making his art ubiquitous in all expressions of eighteenth-century French taste. In 1768, Guillaume-Nicolas Desprez (1713–1795) described Boucher as "varied, fertile and full of invention in all that he undertook, but especially in the agreeable subjects that his natural taste preferred . . . the graces more difficult to grasp than beauty itself reproduce themselves under his brush in a thousand different forms."[18]

The experience of working on a large scale for tapestry designs carried over into two of his largest pastoral paintings: the *Summer Pastoral* (fig. 20) and *Autumn Pastoral* (fig. 21), both of which were created for the chateau of Daniel-Charles Trudaine (1703–1769), at Montigny-Lencoup, near Versailles.[19] Though much grander in format, the two canvases anticipate the themes of two of the Frick *Seasons*. Both depict shepherds in landscapes, with a lake and a round building (similar to those in *Spring* and *Winter*) and a large stone fountain. The shepherdess with her basket of flowers and the shepherd offering his companion some grapes are central to two of the Frick *Seasons* and demonstrate how Boucher played with certain themes and developed them through his career.

The Patron: Madame de Pompadour

Daullé's prints after *The Four Seasons* are all accompanied by the same dedication: "À Madame de Pompadour Dame du Palais de la Reine" (To Madame de Pompadour, Lady-in-Waiting to the Queen). Daullé also specified that the etchings were based on paintings belonging to the dedicatee of the prints: "Le Tableau Original appartient à Madame de Pompadour." (The original painting belongs to Madame de Pompadour). The inscriptions on the sheets provide a key piece of information regarding the original provenance of the four paintings. While the subtly erotic subject matter of the *Seasons* (especially *Summer*) might suggest a male patron, they were made for a woman—"the most charming woman in France," according to King Louis XV.[20]

At the 1757 Salon, Boucher's largest portrait of Madame de Pompadour was prominently exhibited (fig. 22).[21] Portrayed in the afternoon, as shown by the clock reflected in the large mirror in the background, the sitter is in a lavish room decorated with yellow textiles on the walls and matching draperies. In a voluminous green dress, bedecked with pink ribbons and embroidered roses, Pompadour is reclining on a daybed with a book in her hands; more books are in the case that can be seen in the reflection. A small writing table stands to the right—its drawer open—and a sealed letter placed on top of it. At bottom left, Mimi, the sitter's black spaniel, sits among musical scores, prints, drawings, and two pink roses. The magnificent portrait is one of two that were exhibited during Pompadour's life, the other being the large pastel by Maurice-Quentin de La Tour (1704–1788) shown in 1755.[22] Boucher was a reluctant and infrequent portraitist, but over the years he created at least

Following pages:

Fig. 20
François Boucher
Summer Pastoral (Pastoral with a Bagpipe Player), 1749
Oil on canvas
102 × 77 9/16 in. (259 × 197 cm)
The Wallace Collection, London

Fig. 21
François Boucher
Autumn Pastoral (Pastoral with a Couple near a Fountain), 1749
Oil on canvas
102 3/16 × 78 3/16 in.
(259.5 × 198.6 cm)
The Wallace Collection, London

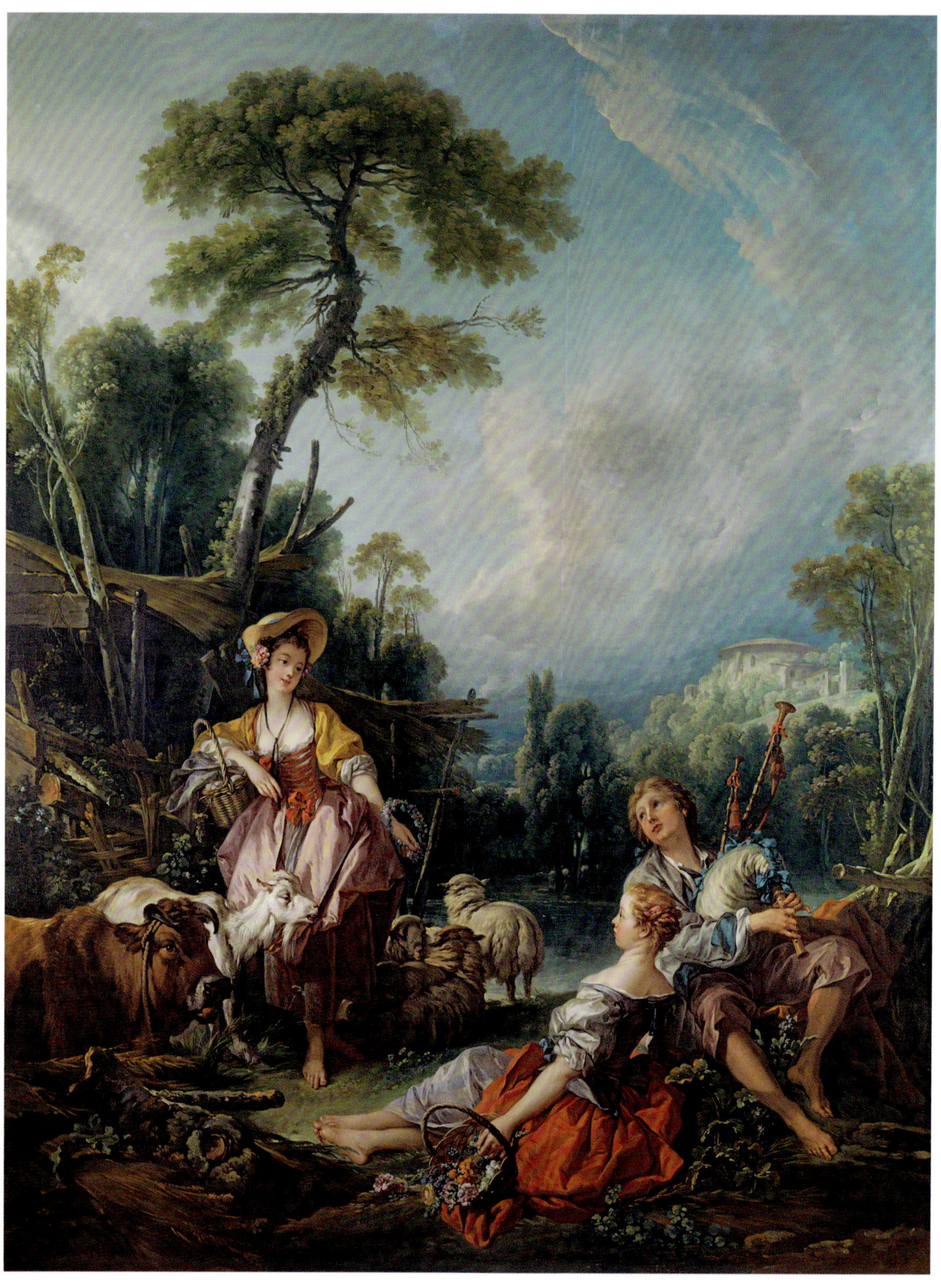

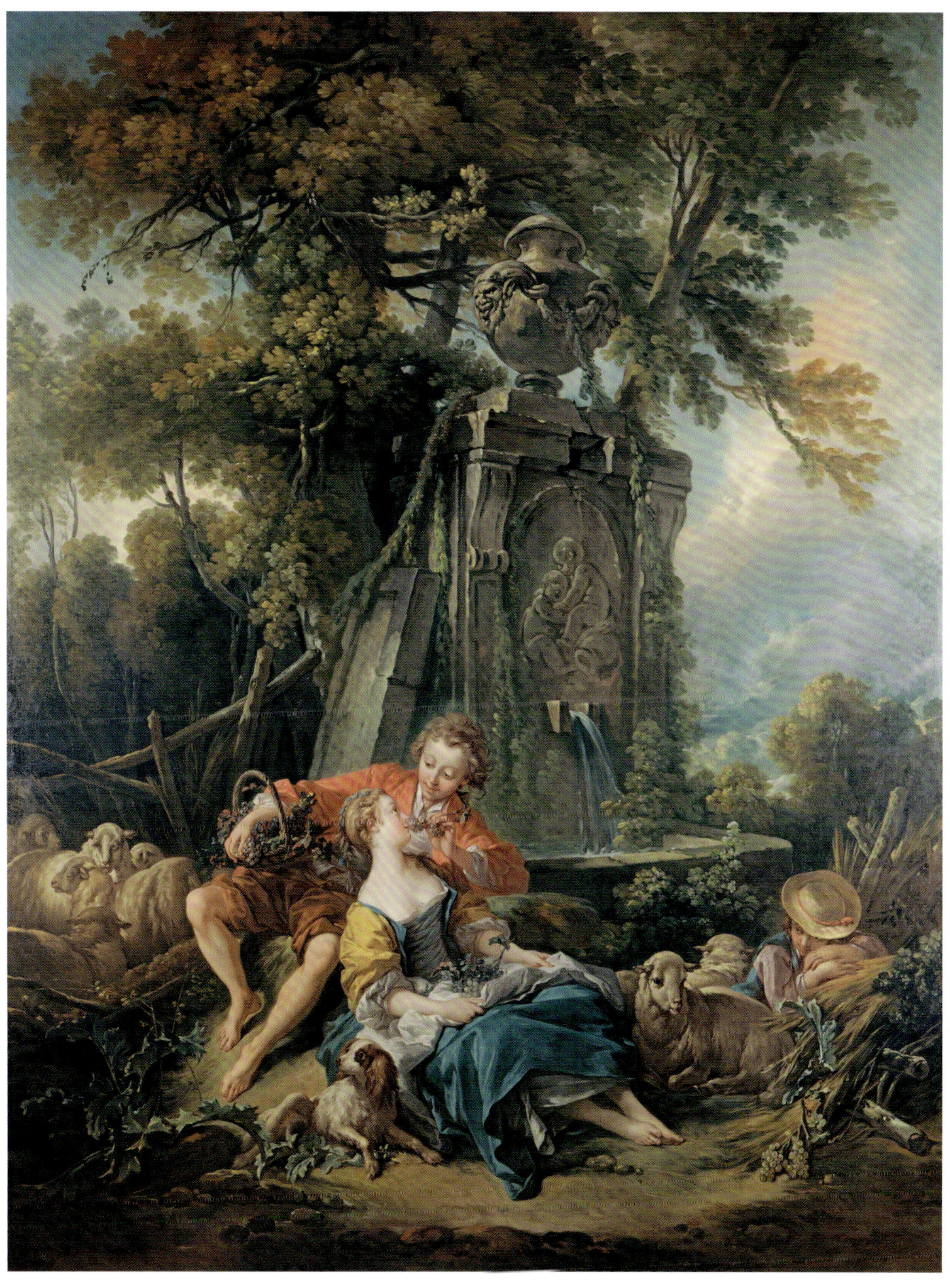

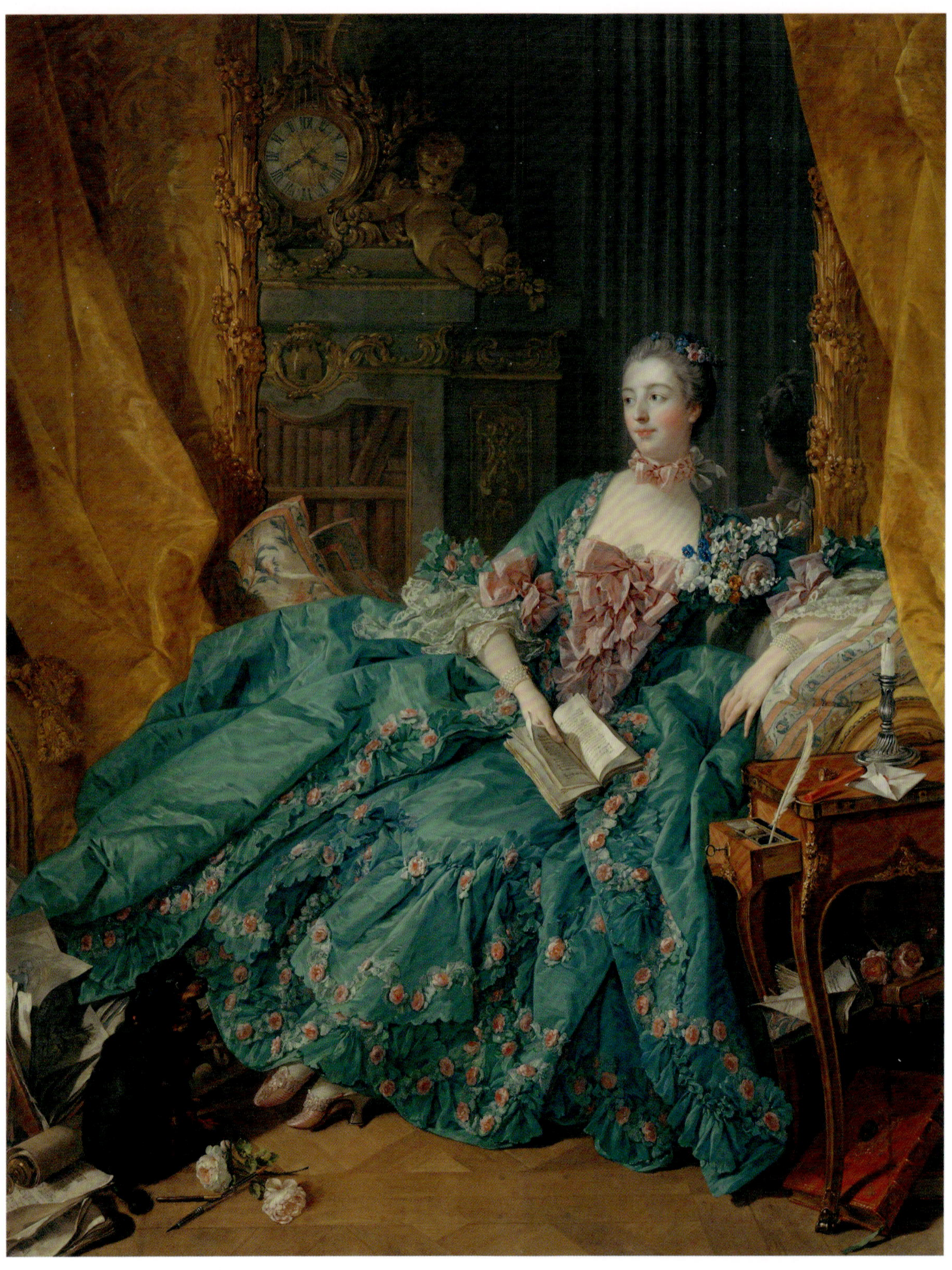

six likenesses of the royal mistress, in which she appears, as described by her contemporaries:

> taller than average, slim, graceful, supple, elegant; her face well matched to her height, of a perfect oval, with beautiful light brown hair, quite large eyes, with fine eyebrows of the same color, the nose perfectly well-formed, the mouth charming . . . the most beautiful skin in the world rendered all her traits all the more striking. Her eyes have a particular charm, which perhaps derives from their uncertain color . . . the ensemble of her person seems to hover between the last degree of elegance and the first of nobility.[23]

Born Jeanne-Antoinette Poisson, in Paris, on December 29, 1721, Pompadour was the daughter of a middle-class businessman, François Poisson (1684–1754), and his wife, Louise-Madeleine de La Motte (1699–1745), reputed for having liaisons with powerful men.[24] The Poissons moved in the circles of the four Pâris brothers, who came from a Grenoble banking family. Madame Poisson was in the midst of an affair with Charles-François Lenormant de Tournehem (1684–1751), a *fermier général* (tax collector) and director of the Compagnie des Indes—said by some to have been the father of Jeanne-Antoinette (others assumed she was the daughter of one of the Pâris brothers)—when, in 1726, a financial scandal cut her husband's career short. Poisson left for Germany in what became an eight-year exile, leaving his wife and children behind, in the care of Lenormant de Tournehem. Between the ages of five and eight, Jeanne-Antoinette lived and studied at the Ursuline convent at Poissy. It is said to have been foretold when she was a young girl, by a certain Madame Lebon, that she would spend her life with the king. For this reason, she was nicknamed "Reinette." Her early years, however, did not seem to presage such an exalted relationship. On March 9, 1741, Jeanne-Antoinette married Charles-Guillaume Lenormant d'Étioles (1717–1799), Tournehem's nephew, in the Parisian church of Saint-Eustache, and the couple established themselves between the Hôtel de Gesvres, on rue Croix-des-Petits-Champs, and the Château d'Étioles. The new Madame d'Étioles swiftly became renowned for her beauty, intelligence, and charm in the literary and theatrical circles of Parisian middle-class and aristocratic society.

Louis XV (fig. 23) had reigned since the death of his great-grandfather, Louis XIV (1638–1715), when he was only five years old. After a brief engagement to a Spanish infanta, Louis married the Polish princess Maria

Fig. 22
François Boucher
Madame de Pompadour, 1756
Oil on canvas
80 11/16 × 63 3/8 in. (205 × 161 cm)
HypoVereinsbank, Member
of UniCredit, on loan
to the Bayerische
Staatsgemäldesammlungen,
Alte Pinakothek, Munich

Fig. 23
Maurice-Quentin de La Tour
Louis XV, 1748
Pastel on paper
25 9/16 × 21 3/8 in. (65 × 54.3 cm)
Musée du Louvre, Paris

Following pages:

Fig. 24
Charles-Nicolas Cochin
Le Bal des Ifs (The Ball of the
Yew Trees), 1745
Ink and watercolor on paper
17 3/4 × 29 15/16 in.
(450 × 760 mm)
Musée du Louvre, Département
des Arts Graphiques, Paris

Leszczyńska (1703–1768), in September 1725. In the early 1730s, after a few happy years and the birth of a number of children, Louis began to have affairs with women at court. For a decade, his mistresses were—one after another—three sisters of the Nesle family: Louise, comtesse de Mailly (1710–1751); Pauline, marquise de Vintimille (1712–1741); and Marie-Anne, duchesse de Châteauroux (1717–1744). It was the custom of the kings of France to have official mistresses (*maîtresses-en-titre*), women who were typically members of noble families and figures in the courtly circles.

When the duchesse de Châteauroux died, in 1744, few at Versailles would have guessed that the new official companion of the king would be a bourgeoise like Madame d'Étioles instead of a fourth Nesle sister. By 1745, it seems that Reinette had been spotted a number of times in her colorful carriage by the king during his hunts at Choisy (the Château d'Étioles was conveniently close). In addition to the death of his latest mistress, the king had also suffered the loss of two people who had been substitute parents to him after the deaths of his father, mother, and older brother in the early months of 1712: Cardinal André-Hercule de Fleury (1653–1743), his childhood tutor and long-standing prime minister, and Madame de Ventadour (1654–1744), his governess. Early in 1745, Louis XV and Madame d'Étioles became lovers. The relationship was made public on February 25, 1745, when a lavish ball was organized at Versailles to celebrate the marriage of the dauphin Louis (1729–1765) to the infanta María Teresa of Spain (1726–1746). Dressed as a gardener and a flower-seller, respectively, the bride and groom presided over the masked ball while Madame d'Étioles attended in the guise of the goddess Diana. At the height of the evening, eight figures dressed identically as clipped yew trees in vases appeared (fig. 24). One of the trees was the king, thus disguised so as not to be identified among his fellow yews. Soon, however, it became easy to spot him, as one of the trees spent the entire ball talking to Diana. The ball became known as the Bal des Ifs (Ball of the Yew Trees). A few days later, a ball at the Hôtel de Ville in Paris sealed the union between the king and Reinette. Her ascent was instantaneous: a separation from her husband was promptly arranged, and by July the king had ennobled her and given her the title of marquise de Pompadour. Although she was later made a duchess, she always used the title of marquise. On September 14, she was presented at court to both the king and queen. As the biographer Nancy Mitford observed, "all these signs of power came gradually; gradually the courtiers understood that there were two Queens of France within the walls

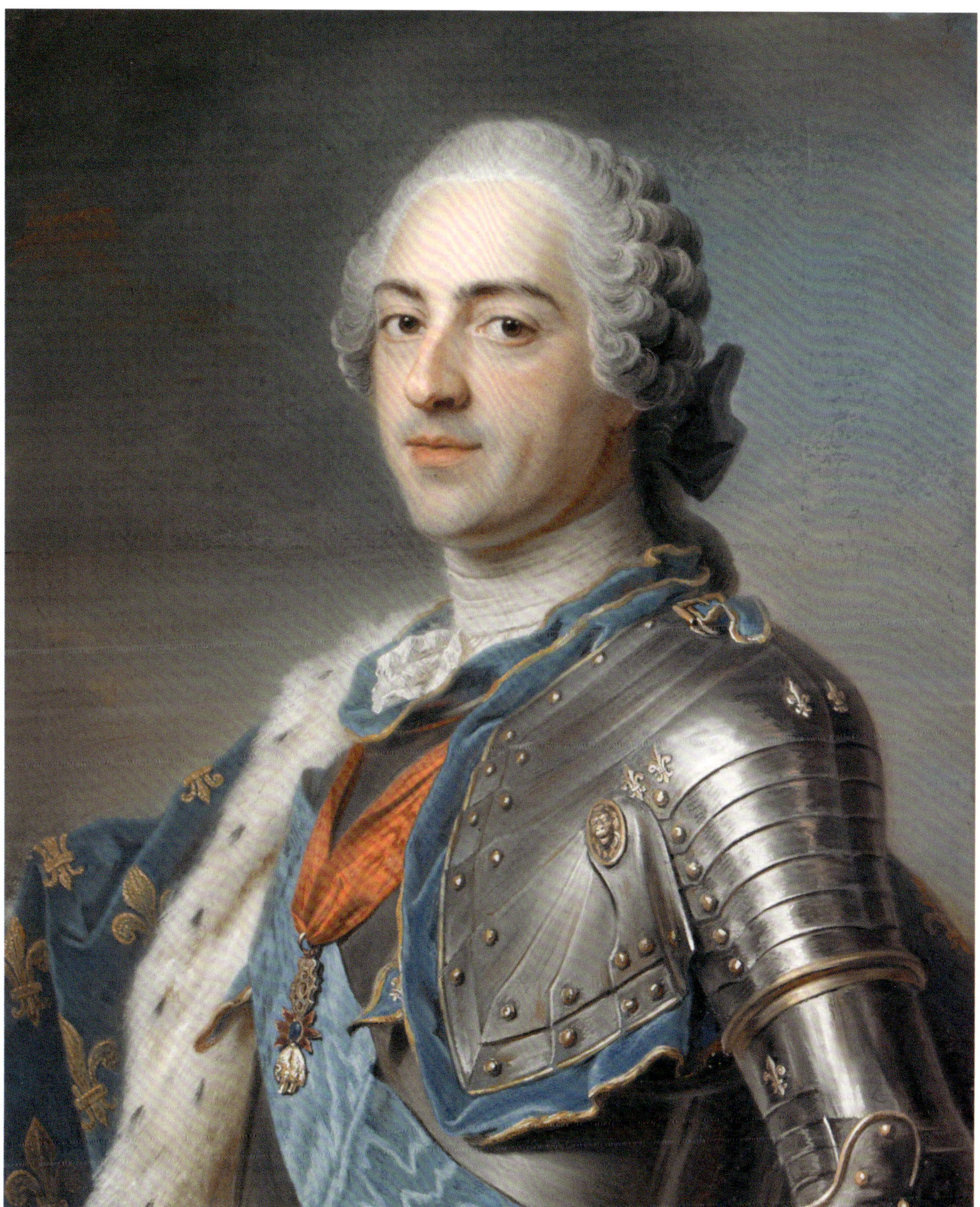

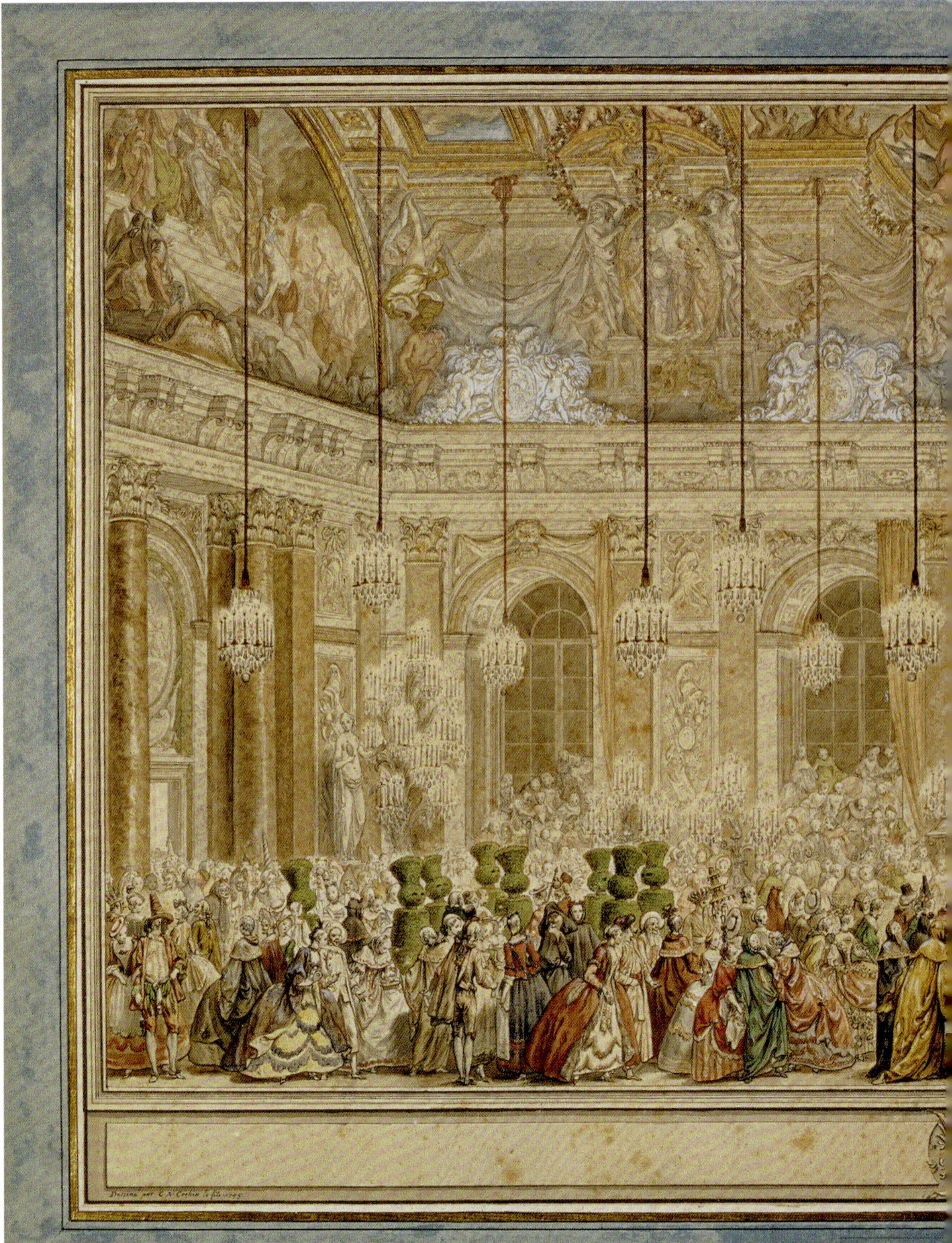

Dessiné par C. N. Cochin le fils 1745
C. N.

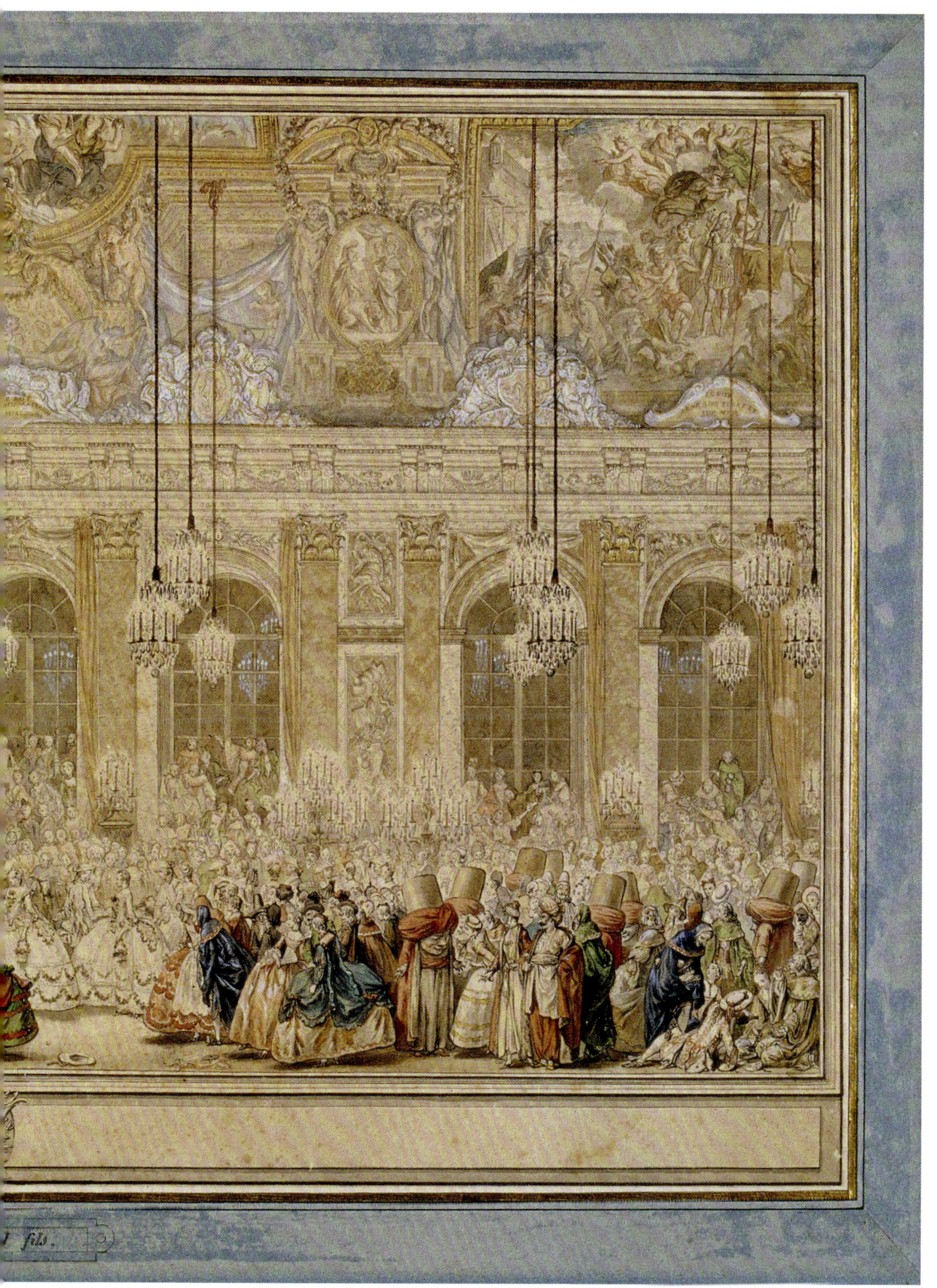
fils.

of Versailles, and that it was not the wife of the King who reigned."[25] For two decades, until her death in 1764, Pompadour was inseparable from the king and a key figure at court. By 1756, when Boucher painted her portrait (exhibited at the Salon a year later) and Daullé etched *The Four Seasons*, Pompadour had obtained the official title of lady-in-waiting to the long-suffering queen, thereby attaining even more prominence at court.

Pompadour, however, was known (and self-described) as a woman with little interest in physical relationships with men, and after the early years of her affair with the king, around the early 1750s, their connection became, by and large, platonic. Nevertheless, she was indispensable to him as a confidante and supporter and remained his official mistress. While the king consoled himself with a series of women of easy virtue who were housed in a royal brothel known as the Parc aux Cerfs, Pompadour remained his emotional and intellectual partner.

The 1750s marked a series of tragedies in the life of both the king and Pompadour. In 1754, the marquise's young daughter (her only surviving child with her husband), Alexandrine, and her father died within four days of each other. In January 1757, the assassination attempt on the king by Robert-François Damiens (1714–1757) threatened the role of Pompadour at court over a period of several days when the life of the king was believed to be in danger. These events were pitted against the broader background of the disastrous Seven Years' War, which saw France lose—alongside Austria and Spain—against Prussia and England: it began in 1756 and concluded a year before Pompadour's death.

The royal mistress's greatest contribution was her promotion of the visual arts.[26] As the British writer and collector William Beckford (1760–1844) observed in 1815: "no lady of the old or new world has ever been a better judge of the rare, the beautiful and the fine than Madame de Pompadour."[27] Mitford reviewed her activities as a collector:

> Madame de Pompadour never seems to have sold any of the objects which belonged to her. They accumulated in their thousands, and filled all her many houses to overflowing; after her death Marigny [Pompadour's brother and heir] was obliged to take two big houses in Paris which, as well as the Elysée and the Réservoirs, contained her goods until the sale of them began. Furniture, china, statues, pictures, books, plants, jewels, linen, silver, carriages, horses, yards and hundreds of yards of stuff, trunks full of dresses, cellars full of wine; the inventory of all this, divided into nearly three

thousand lots, very few lots containing less than a dozen objects, took two lawyers more than a year to make. Few human beings since the world began can have owned so many beautiful things.[28]

Pompadour's interest in the arts was wide-ranging. There was no field in which she was not involved over her two decades at Versailles. When it came to painters, Boucher was clearly her favorite artist. As Mitford observed, Boucher was "as it were official painter to Madame de Pompadour, a position which, he said, he greatly preferred to that of Van Loo who was official painter to the Court."[29]

Boucher and Madame de Pompadour

Jo Hedley has perceptively noted that "Boucher's paintings helped Madame de Pompadour to invest her interiors at Court with something of the luxurious chic and intimacy of the Parisian capital, while in return, her patronage of Boucher clearly singled him out as the first decorative painter of the day."[30] The artist established himself as a favorite of the royal mistress, and, apart from her many portraits, he produced numerous works for her and her several houses. These also ranged in subject matter and size.

The Bath of Venus (fig. 25) and The Toilette of Venus (fig. 26), painted in 1751 for Pompadour, are archetypal Boucher mythological scenes, both focusing on the goddess of love—bathing in a stream, accompanied by cupids, and indoors preparing to dress, also accompanied by cupids.[31] In both paintings, the voluptuous body of Venus is exposed—outdoors in a glade and inside on a daybed in a loggia—in a prominent way, and, like the *Odalisque brune*, the goddesses' nudity is underscored by its juxtaposition with various painted fabrics: rich blue and burgundy velvets and diaphanous silk sheets. The subject matter of the paintings is clearly associated with its patron: the goddess of love would have been an obvious role model for the royal mistress. But the two paintings also relate to their original location. Between the late 1740s and the end of 1750, Pompadour built and lavishly decorated the Château de Bellevue, on the road between Paris and Versailles. The two Boucher canvases were planned for the main room of the three rooms in the *appartement des bains* (bathing apartment), in a structure separate from the main building of the chateau. Both were made to be used as overdoors: *The Bath of Venus* over the door to the actual bathing chamber and the *Toilette* over the door to the dressing

Following pages:

Fig. 25
François Boucher
The Bath of Venus, 1751
Oil on canvas
42⅛ × 33⅛ in. (107 × 84.8 cm)
National Gallery of Art,
Washington

Fig. 26
François Boucher
The Toilette of Venus, 1751
Oil on canvas
42⅝ × 33½ in. (108.3 × 85.1 cm)
The Metropolitan Museum of
Art, New York

Fig. 27
François Boucher
The Rising of the Sun, 1753
Oil on canvas
125³⁄₁₆ × 102¾ in.
(318 × 261 cm)
The Wallace Collection, London

Fig. 28
François Boucher
The Setting of the Sun, 1752
Oil on canvas
125³⁄₁₆ × 102¾ in.
(318 × 261 cm)
The Wallace Collection, London

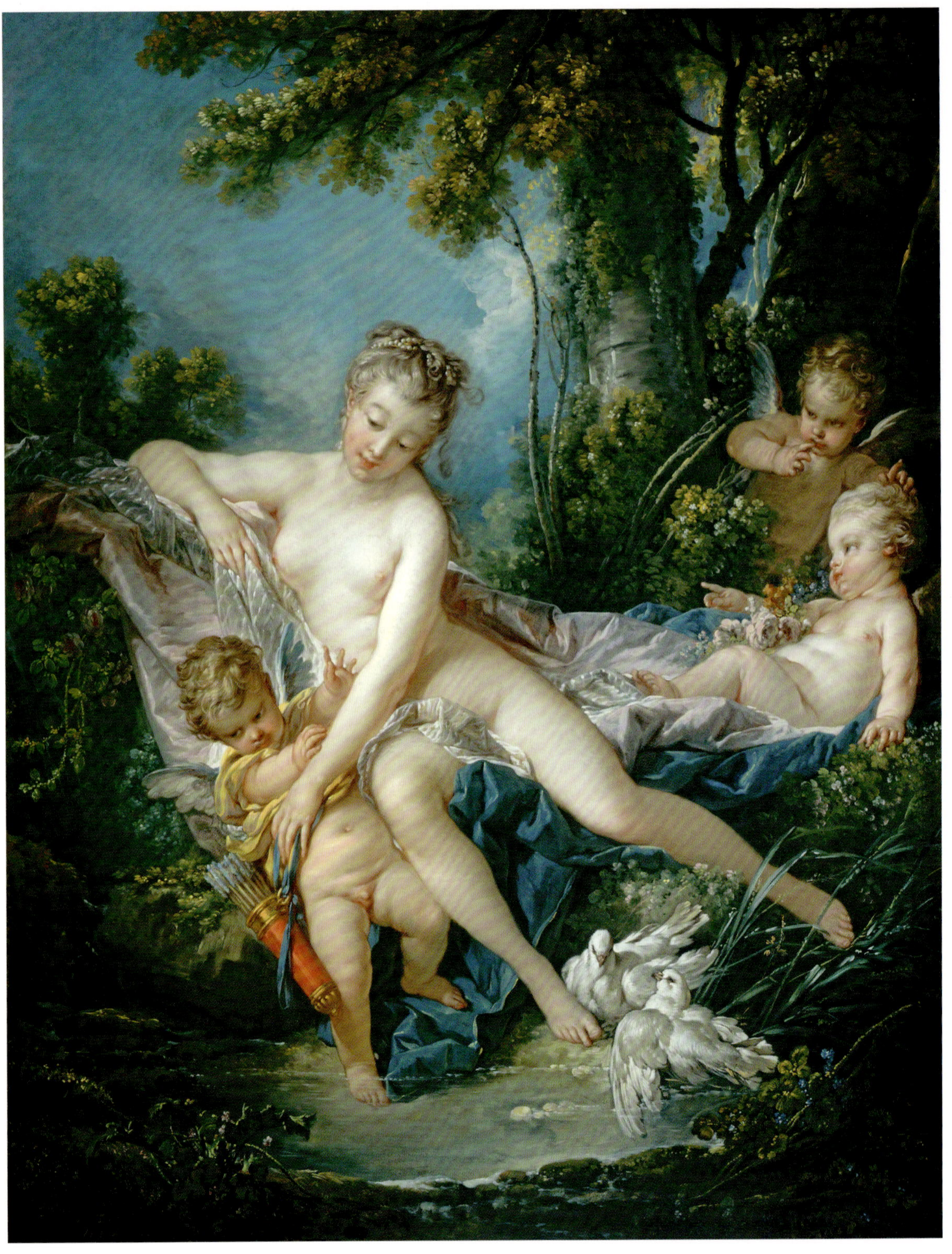

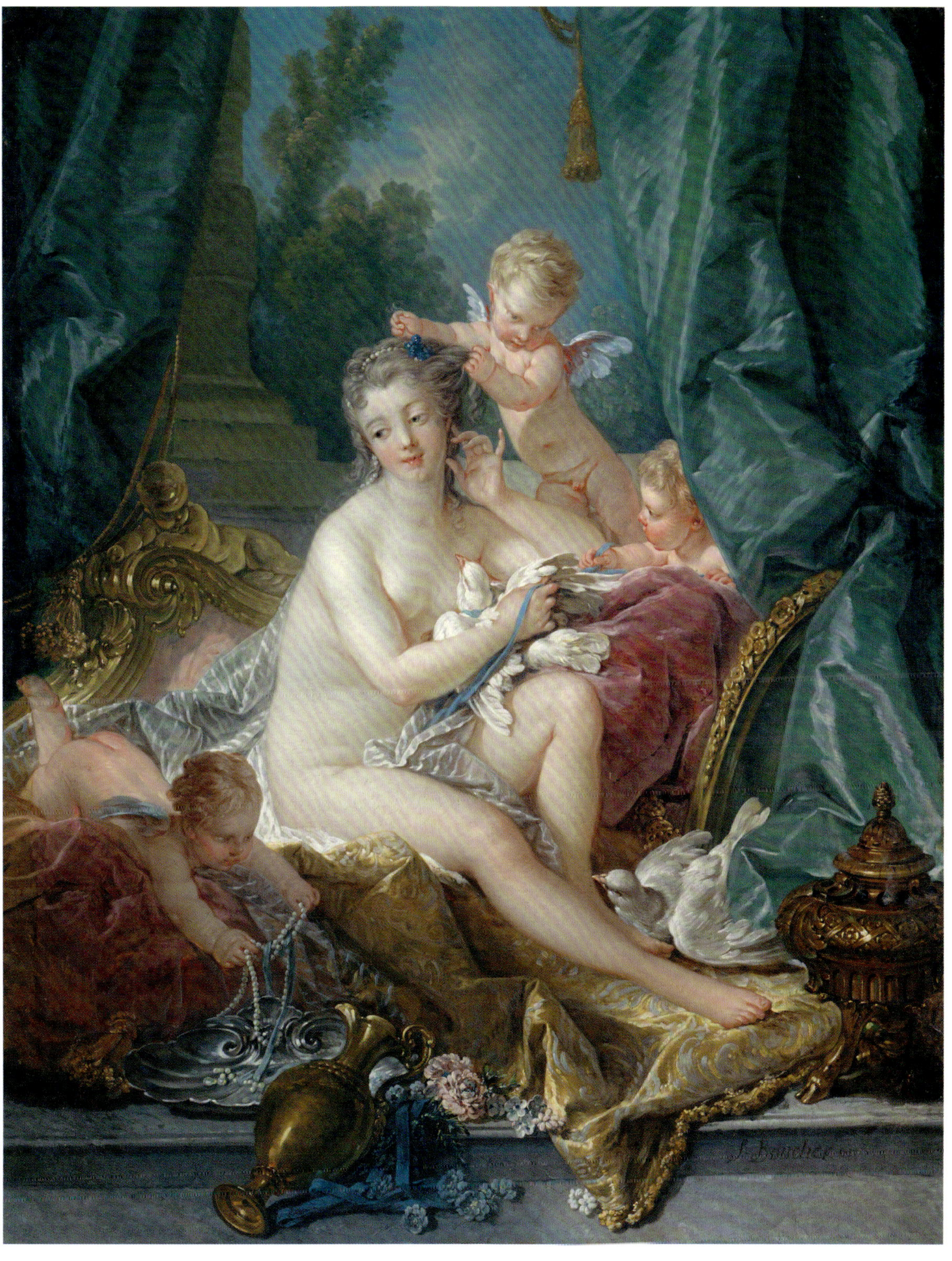

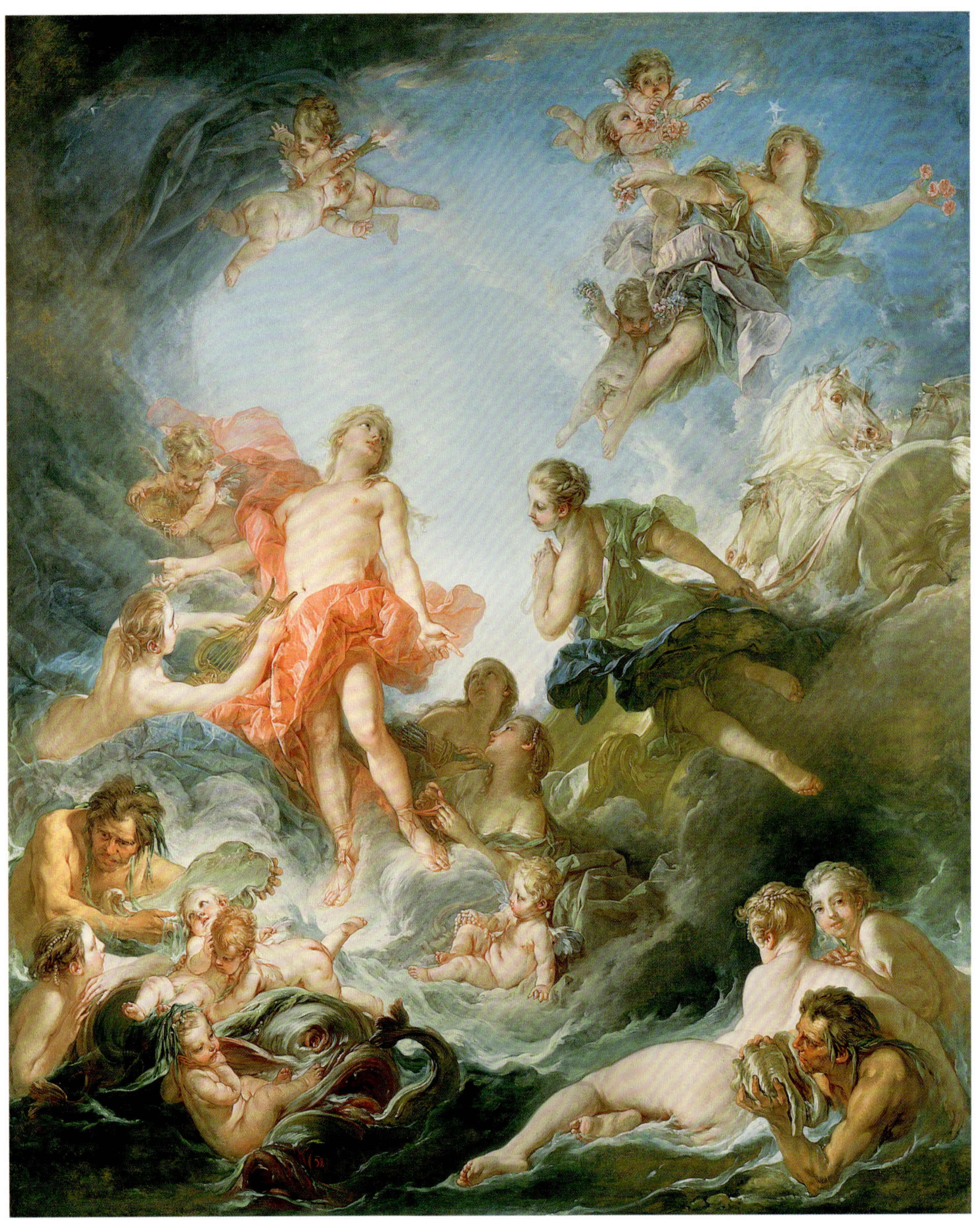

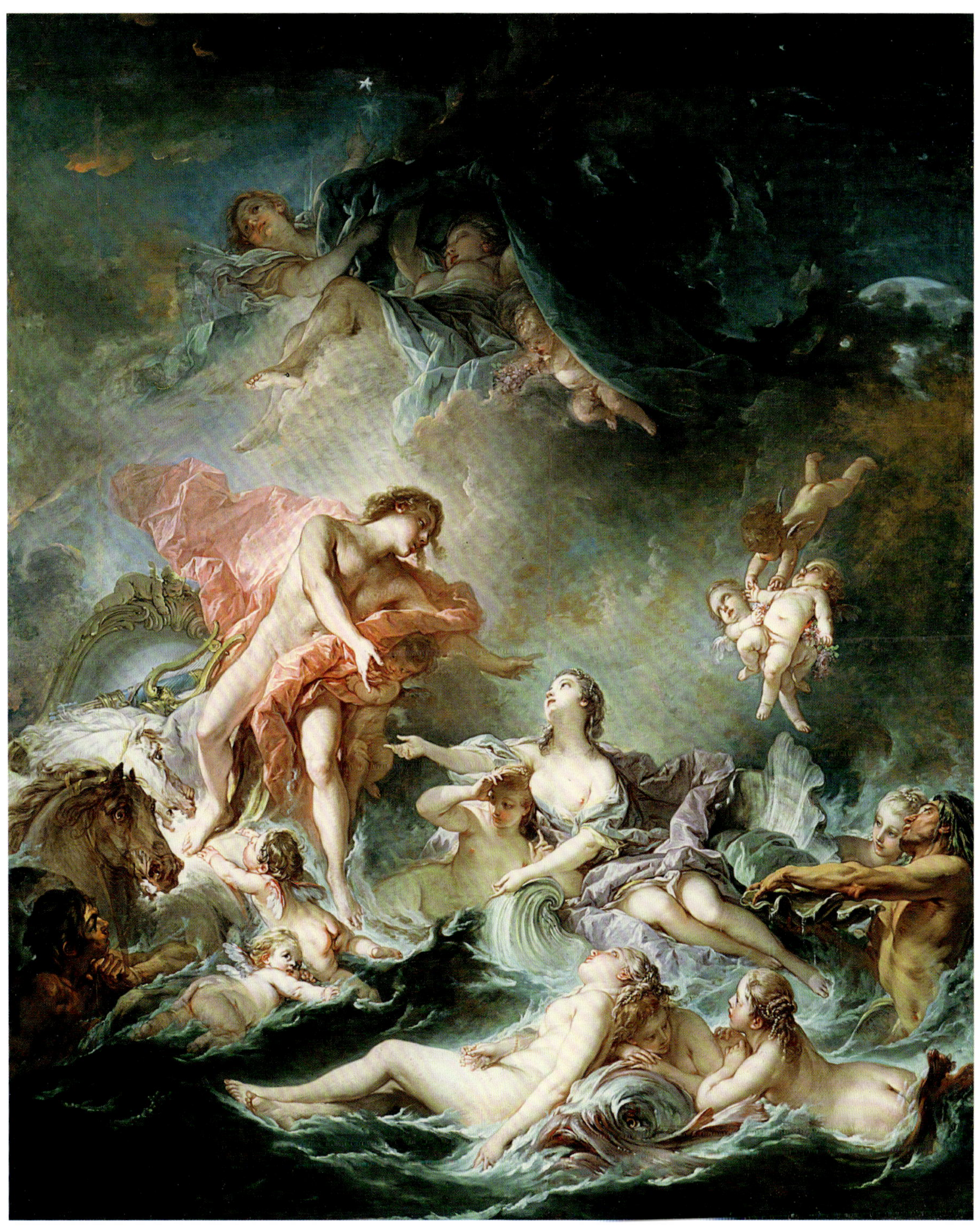

Fig. 29
François Boucher
La Lumière du monde (The
Light of the World), 1750
Oil on canvas
69 × 51 in. (175 × 130 cm)
Musée des Beaux-Arts, Lyon

room. Boucher clearly considered both whom he was painting the work for and where it was to be displayed. In 1757, Pompadour sold the chateau to the king and moved its contents to her Parisian residence—the Hôtel d'Evreux (today's presidential palace of the Élysée)—where they were at her death, in 1764.

Two other pendant canvases by Boucher, much larger than the *Bath* and *Toilette of Venus*, were painted in 1752–53, also for Bellevue. Pompadour had commissioned Boucher to design a set of tapestries—which were produced by the Gobelins manufactory—for the king's bedroom on the second floor at Bellevue. The two main tapestries, for which Boucher created large painted canvases as cartoons, were *The Rising of the Sun* (fig. 27) and *The Setting of the Sun* (fig. 28), which were exhibited at the Salon of 1753.[32] Pompadour acquired the canvases so that no additional versions of the two tapestries could be produced. The canvases were installed on the first floor at Bellevue in the Salon of the Swiss Guards, the king's bodyguards. The two monumental paintings, among Boucher's masterpieces, depict the god Apollo rising and setting, defining the beginning and end of the infinite cycle of days, accompanied by Aurora (Dawn), the Morning and Evening Stars, Tethys and nymphs and tritons. It would not have been difficult to identify the figure of Apollo and of the sun with Louis XV. The rising and setting of the sun would have been particularly appropriate for the king's bedroom, where he would have officially begun and finished his days at Bellevue in the elaborate public ceremonies of the rising (*lever*) and setting (*coucher*) of the king.

For Bellevue, Boucher also painted, in 1750, a canvas of a very different subject: the so-called *Lumière du monde* (Light of the World) (fig. 29).[33] The large painting depicts a traditional Christian narrative, the Adoration of the Shepherds after the birth of Christ in Bethlehem. Under a glory of divine light and cherubs, the Virgin presents the baby Jesus to a group of shepherds and shepherdesses who bring gifts of eggs, chickens, and doves. The scene is not, however, a straightforward Adoration of the Shepherds. In the background, on the left, the figure of an old, bearded man seems to be Joseph, Mary's husband, who is present in any Nativity scene. The figure is accompanied by an ox, one of two animals—along with a donkey—traditionally associated with scenes of the birth of Christ. Yet, looking carefully at the detail of the painting, it appears that while the ox is shown, there is no donkey, and that the old man is writing in a large book next to the animal. The man is, therefore, not Joseph but rather Luke the Evangelist (whose symbol is an ox). And the painting can

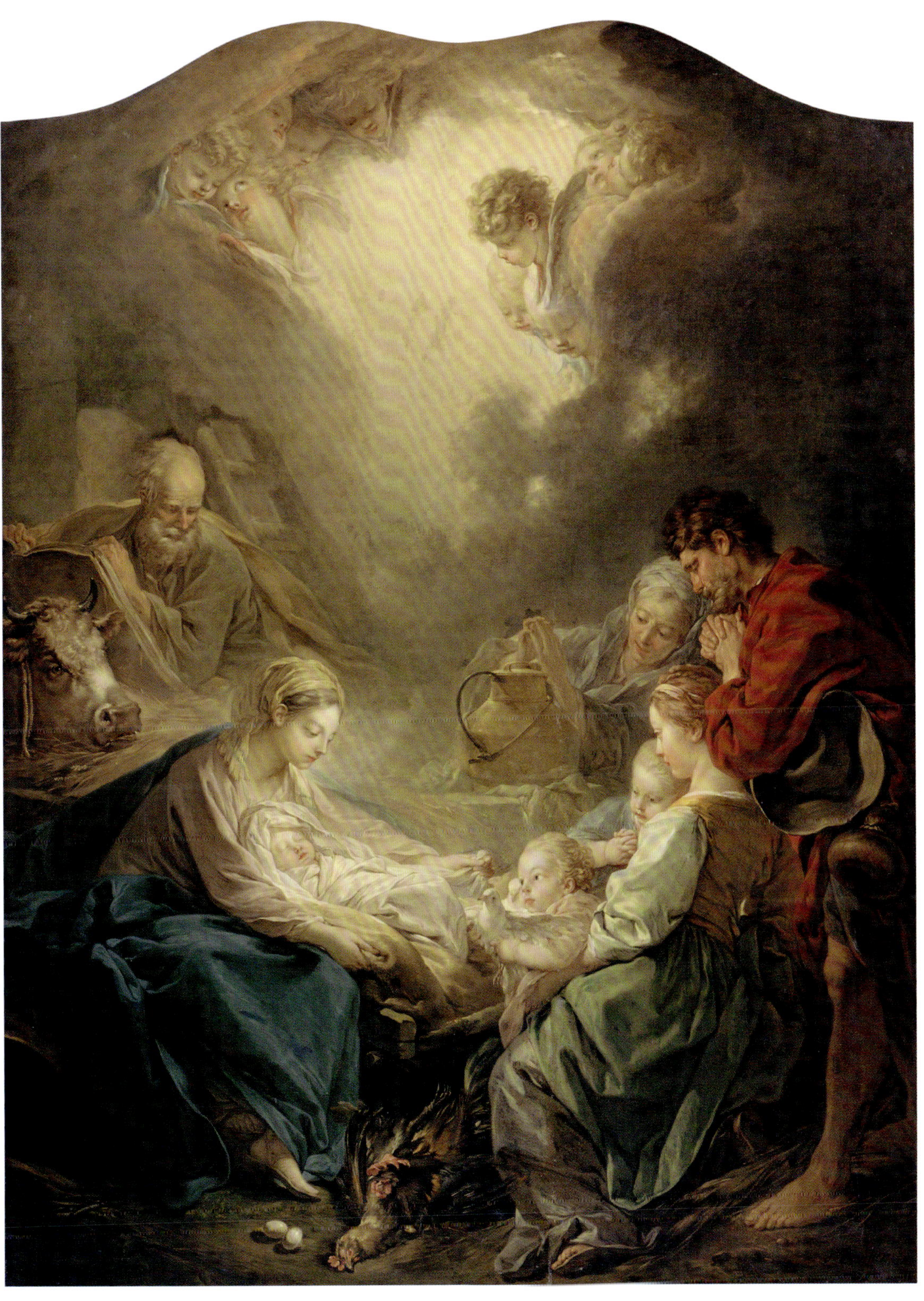

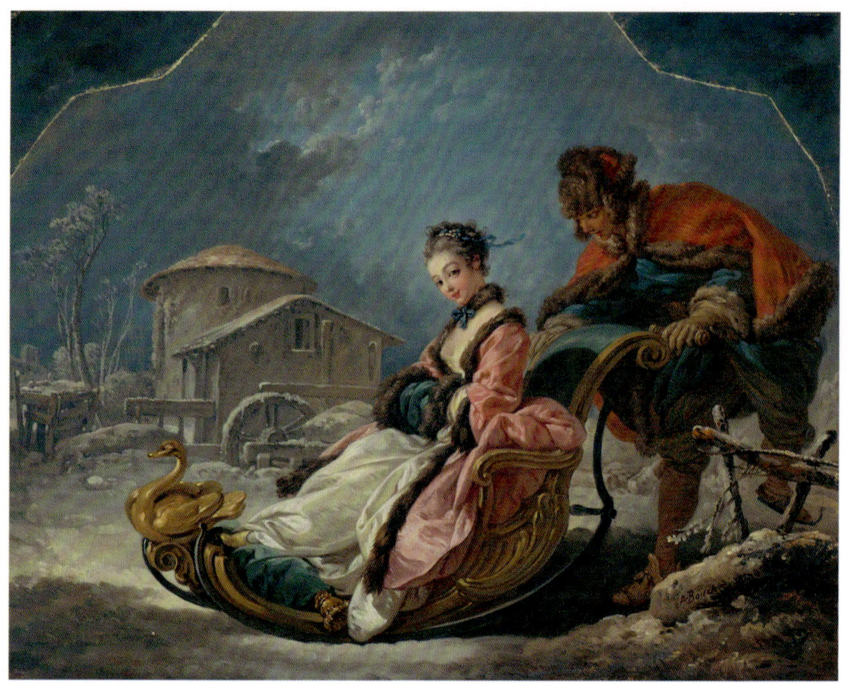

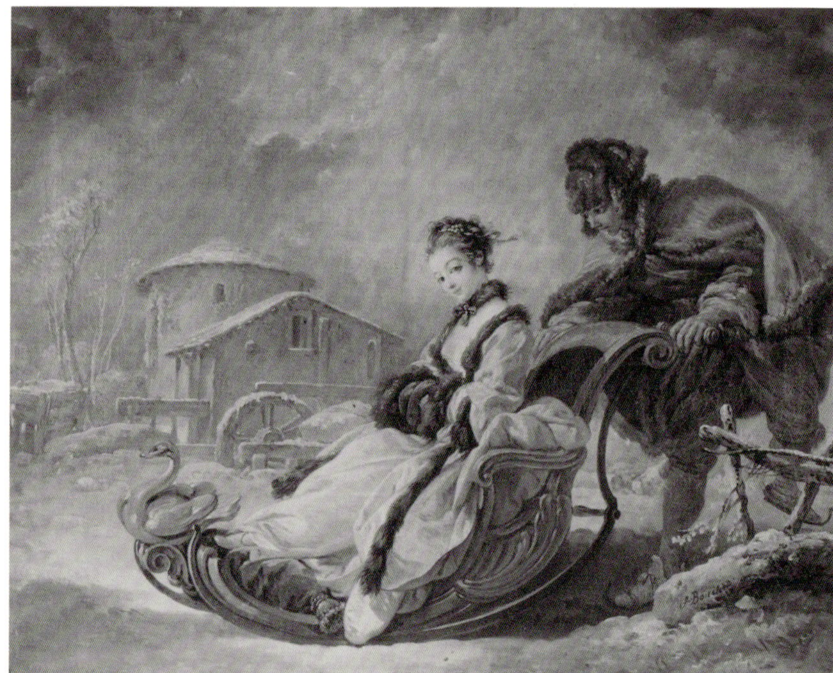

Fig. 30
Photo of Boucher's *Four Seasons: Winter*, unframed 2024. The Frick Collection, New York

Fig. 31
Photo of Boucher's *Four Seasons: Winter*, showing it as a rectangle. The Frick Collection, New York

be explained by a passage in the Gospel of Luke (2:32): "A light to lighten the Gentiles, and the glory of thy people Israel." Boucher's painting was intended to serve as an altarpiece. As there was no chapel at Bellevue, the Boucher altarpiece was placed in a large cupboard in an anteroom. The cupboard could be opened and the anteroom used as a chapel or kept closed when the room was to be used in a different way.

Boucher and Pompadour had a close relationship. Boucher taught the royal mistress the art of etching, which she enjoyed, and also provided her with set designs for her theatrical productions to entertain the king, especially at Bellevue.

The Original Location and Purpose of *The Four Seasons*

Between October 1944 and March 1945, the restorer Gaston Levi cleaned the Frick's *Four Seasons*.[34] When Henry Clay Frick purchased the paintings, they were rectangular in shape (fig. 31); and the prints by Daullé depict them as rectangles (see figs. 6, 8, 10, 12). However, the restoration revealed that the four canvases originally had an irregular shape, the corners having been extended and filled in to make them into rectangles (fig. 30). It is impossible to establish whether the canvases were originally rectangular, then cut into an irregular shape and later restored as rectangles, or if they were envisioned with irregular shapes to begin with. It is likely, however, that the four paintings did initially have an irregular shape and that the corners are later additions.[35] A comparison with two other works by Boucher made for Pompadour is instructive.

In 1750, the painter made the canvases *Le Sommeil interrompu* (The Interrupted Sleep) (fig. 32) and *Les Deux Confidentes* (The Two Confidantes or The Love Letter) (fig. 33) as overdoors for a room at the Château de Bellevue.[36] The two canvases depict pastoral subjects: a young shepherd tickling with a piece of straw a young shepherdess who has fallen asleep under a tree after gathering flowers in a basket, and two shepherdesses sitting under the sculpture of a lion sending (or receiving?) a love letter secured with a string to a white dove. Though created for Bellevue, both paintings were transferred in 1757 to the Hôtel d'Evreux, where they were described in 1764. When they entered the collections of the museums in New York and Washington, they were rectangular in shape; again, prints after them show them as rectangular. The cleaning of the New York canvas showed clearly that the corners were added—and the same can be seen in the Washington one when examining it

Following pages:

Fig. 32
François Boucher
Le Sommeil interrompu (The Interrupted Sleep), 1750
Oil on canvas
32¼ × 29⅝ in. (81.9 × 75.2 cm)
The Metropolitan Museum of Art, New York

Fig. 33
François Boucher
Les Deux Confidentes (The Two Confidantes or The Love Letter), 1750
Oil on canvas
31¹⁵⁄₁₆ × 29⅝ in. (81.2 × 75.2 cm)
National Gallery of Art, Washington

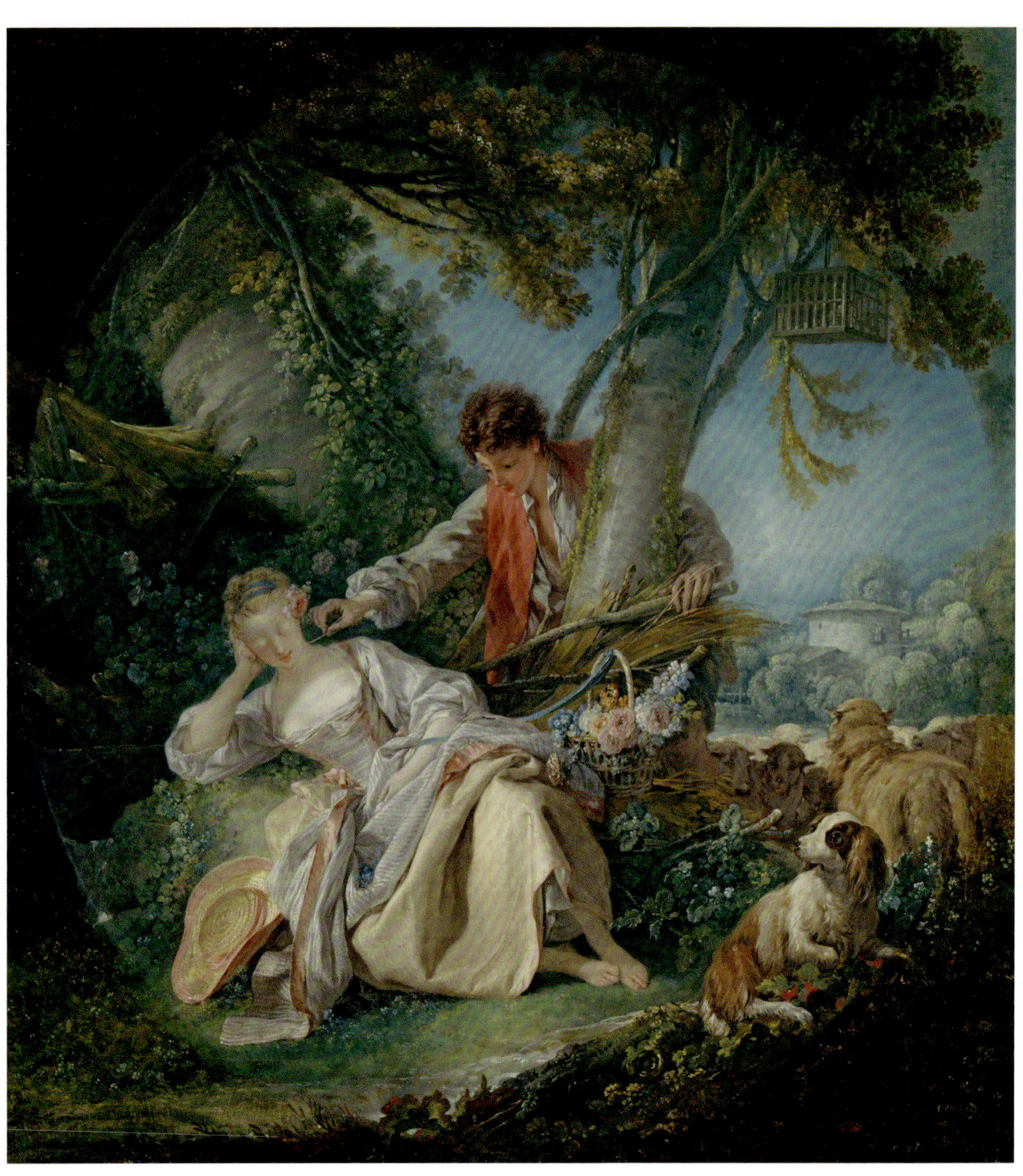

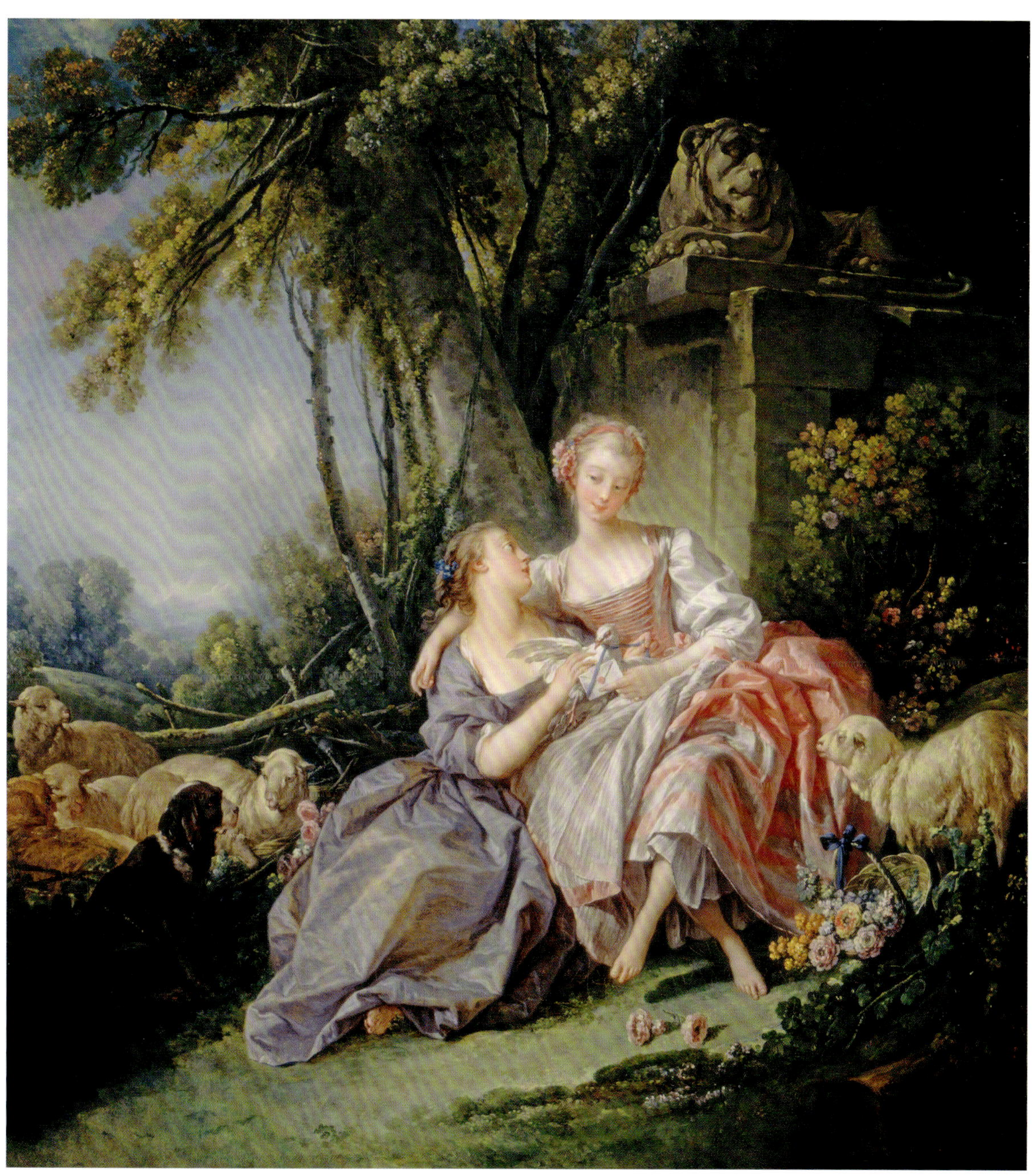

properly. X-rays of *The Interrupted Sleep* have also shown, however, that the canvases were not symmetrical ovals to begin with but rather—like the Frick *Four Seasons*—irregular in shape and clearly made with a specific site in mind.

Canvases with curvilinear, scalloped shapes, known in French as *tableaux chantournés*, were often produced in eighteenth-century France, especially by Boucher. This was typical of works made to be installed into wood paneling (*boiseries*) decorating rooms of elegant interiors.[37] Canvases of this shape were often meant to serve as overdoors, as was the case with a number of Boucher works (see, for example, figs. 17–18 and 32–33). Once the canvases were removed from their original settings, no longer serving as overdoors, and once they entered the art market, they were given rectangular shapes.[38] This seems to have happened to many works by Boucher. Surprisingly, *chantourné* canvases were often displayed at the Salon in their irregular shapes before being placed in the *boiseries* for which they were intended. However, if they were engraved (as in the case of *The Four Seasons*), the printmaker would always regularize their shape in the prints to make the sheets more marketable.

Given their original *chantourné* shape (now suggested by the way they are framed) and their dimensions, the Frick's *Four Seasons* were almost certainly intended to be overdoors. In 1891, the journalist Louis Énault wrote that the canvases may have served as overdoors, and later scholars followed his lead.[39] Aside from the inscriptions in Daullé's prints, unfortunately, no evidence survives to link *The Four Seasons* to a specific location or a building belonging to Madame de Pompadour. Pierre de Nolhac, in 1905, proposed that "they were originally intended to decorate an elegant room of medium size, which seems to have been found in one of Madame de Pompadour's residences"; which residence, however, cannot be determined.[40] The marquise had many houses over her twenty years at the king's side. She, of course, had apartments at Versailles, close to the king's private quarters—between 1745 and 1751 on the top floor, and between 1751 and 1764 on the ground floor. She had apartments in many of the royal residences—at Fontainebleau, Trianon, and Compiègne—and also had small follies in some of these parks: the hermitages of Versailles, Compiègne, and Fontainebleau. There was her main Parisian residence, the Hôtel d'Evreux, and her Hôtel des Réservoirs at Versailles, as well as her other, larger and smaller, houses at Crécy, Bellevue, Auvilliers, Brimborian, Montretout, La Celle, Saint-Ouen, and Menars.[41] Most of these sites have been destroyed or altered beyond recognition. Pompadour would decorate a space, only to move on to a different residence and begin decorating all over again. As we have seen with some of the Boucher paintings made for Bellevue and then relocated to the Hôtel d'Evreux, she often moved works of art from one residence to another.

After her death, a complete inventory of all her belongings was compiled; it took more than a year—from June 1764 to July 1765—to finish it. Strangely, Boucher's *Four Seasons* do not appear in any of the inventories of Pompadour's belongings.[42] Georges Brunel believed that they "may have been the overdoors installed" in the royal residence at "Choisy in 1755," but this is not supported by any firm evidence.[43] The fact that they were installed as part of the *boiserie* of a room and therefore were, to some degree, not movable, may explain why they were not described in inventories (even though overdoors do appear in similar documents and others are described in Pompadour's inventories). Many works by Boucher are mentioned in the inventory, including paintings, drawings, and pastels by him, but the inventory also includes tapestries, furniture, porcelain, and prints based on designs by Boucher.[44] In some instances, overdoors are described but their author not mentioned, as, for example, in the following entry: "with regard to four overdoors, painted on canvas, representing different subjects, they were not prized, but only recorded for Memory" in a bedroom in the Hôtel d'Evreux in Paris.[45] More recently, Colin Bailey has argued that *The Four Seasons* "are rather small to have been placed high above doors or pier glasses. Perhaps they were set into the paneling of a small room at eye level or just above; at the very least, the care Boucher took in executing them would indicate that they were destined for an intimate chamber, a *cabinet* perhaps."[46] Where this space would have been remains unknown.

Pompadour's *Seasons*

The subject of *The Four Seasons* would have been particularly appropriate for one of Pompadour's residences, which were surrounded by gardens. All four paintings are set in landscapes and can be envisioned in a room looking out onto gardens. The marquise was known for her love of gardens and flowers. Mitford described this taste when writing about her small house on the grounds at Versailles:

> The great point of the Hermitage was its wonderful garden, all arranged
> for scent so that one heavenly smell led to another; it could be visited

Fig. 34
François Boucher
Spring, 1753
Oil on canvas
78¾ × 59¹⁄₁₆ in. (200 × 150 cm)
Musée du Louvre, Paris, on long-term loan to the Musée National du Château de Fontainebleau, Fontainebleau

Fig. 35
François Boucher
Summer, 1753
Oil on canvas
78¾ × 59¹⁄₁₆ in. (200 × 150 cm)
Musée du Louvre, Paris, on long-term loan to the Musée National du Château de Fontainebleau, Fontainebleau

Fig. 36
François Boucher
Autumn, 1753
Oil on canvas
78¾ × 59¹⁄₁₆ in. (200 × 150 cm)
Musée du Louvre, Paris, on long-term loan to the Musée National du Château de Fontainebleau, Fontainebleau

Fig. 37
François Boucher
Winter, 1753
Oil on canvas
78¾ × 59¹⁄₁₆ in. (200 × 150 cm)
Musée du Louvre, Paris, on long-term loan to the Musée National du Château de Fontainebleau, Fontainebleau

blindfolded for the scent alone. Here she had fifty orange trees, lemons, oleanders single and double, myrtle, olives, yellow jasmine and lilac from Judea, and pomegranates, all in straight avenues with trellised palisades leading to a bower of roses surrounding a marble Apollo. Shrubs and flowers were brought to Madame de Pompadour from all parts of the French empire, chosen for the scent; she specially loved myrtle, tuberoses, jasmine, and gardenias. Labor was so cheap that flowers in the gardens were renewed every day, as we renew them now in a room; in the greenhouses at Trianon there were two million pots for bedding out.[47]

It is easy to understand how paintings such as Boucher's *Four Seasons* would have appealed to Pompadour, with their outdoor settings and attention to flowers and fountains.

Boucher's relationship to nature seems to have been less straightforward. Allegedly citing a letter to Nicolas Lancret, in 1843 Arsène Houssaye reported that Boucher "found nature extremely disagreeable, too green and badly lit."[48] As noted by Mark Ledbury, however, "this quote has neither been confirmed nor reliably sourced by subsequent scholarship, yet it lives on, irresistible and ubiquitous."[49] Denis Diderot (1713–1784), writing about a painting by Boucher of Angelica and Medoro, exhibited at the Salon of 1765, harshly described how in the background the trees seemed to be covered in parsley.[50] Boucher's pastorals, influenced by Watteau and Lancret's *fête galante* genre, were particularly appreciated by Pompadour and other patrons at the time.[51]

In using the pastoral theme for *Spring* and *Autumn*, a variation of the mythological/erotic for *Summer*, and an almost contemporary genre scene for *Winter*, Boucher was using sources he had already adopted in paintings, embracing previously painted subjects to create a set of four canvases, at first sight consistent as a group but on closer observation different from one another. Only two years before painting them, in 1753, Boucher had contributed to the decoration of the Salle du Conseil (Royal Council Chamber) at Fontainebleau, by providing canvases for its ceiling.[52] The central painting depicts Apollo in his chariot, while in the corners Boucher included frolicking children set in clouds against the blue sky. Each of the four octagonal canvases includes between five and six children accompanied by attributes of the seasons: flowers and doves for *Spring* (fig. 34), wheat and a sickle for *Summer* (fig. 35), a garland of grapes and fruit for *Autumn* (fig. 36), and snow descending from dark clouds for *Winter* (fig. 37). Pompadour would have known these paintings from Fontainebleau.

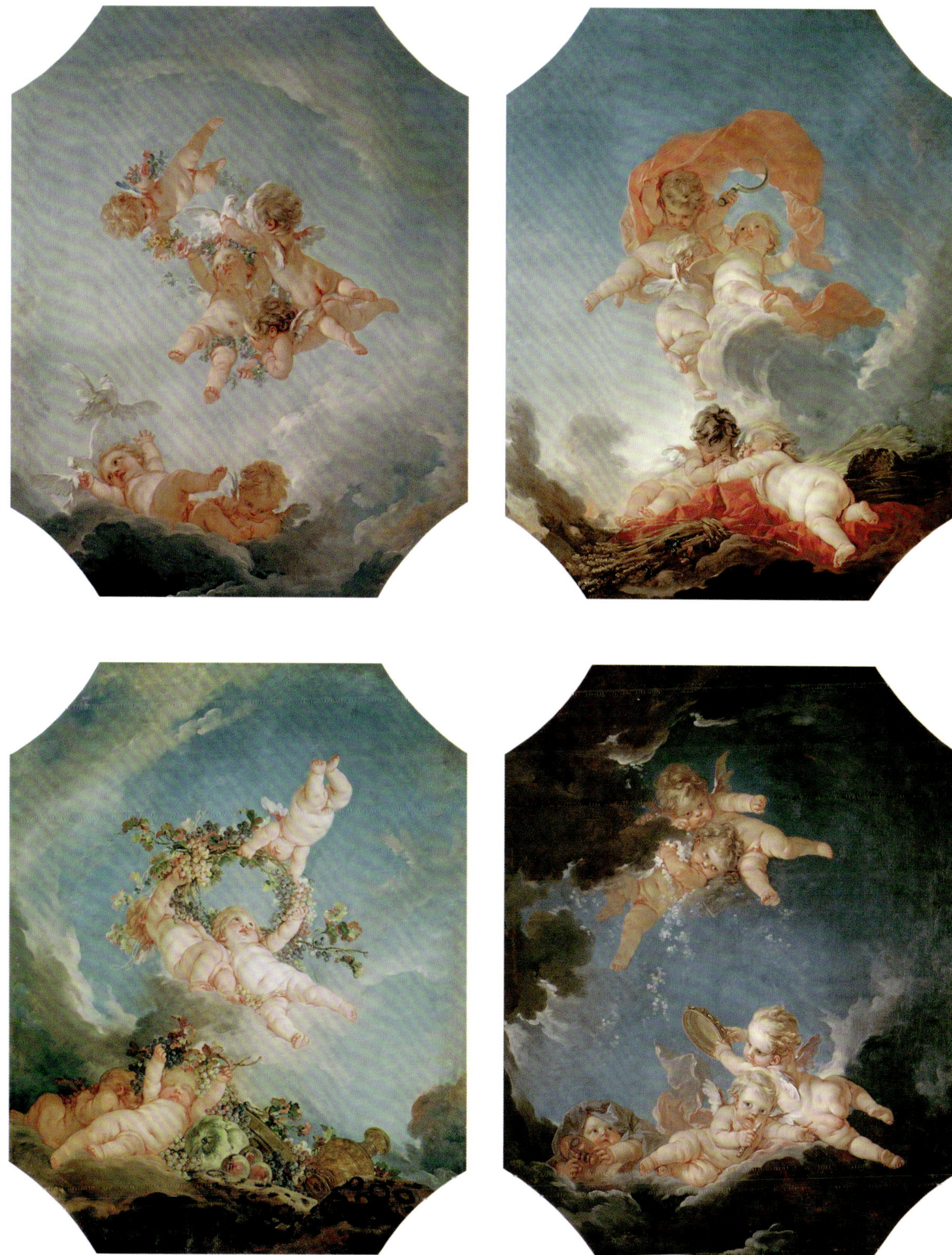

Fig. 38
Louis Tocqué
Abel-François Poisson, Marquis de Marigny, 1755
Oil on canvas
53⅛ × 40¹⁵⁄₁₆ in. (135 × 104 cm)
Musée National des Châteaux de Versailles et de Trianon

They had also been shown at the Salon of 1753 together with the *Rising* (see fig. 27) and the *Setting of the Sun* (see fig. 28) for Bellevue. It is possible that the idea of including the seasons in the decorative scheme at Fontainebleau for the king prompted Pompadour to use the same subjects—albeit depicted in an altogether different fashion—for one of her residences.

To further strengthen the link between Boucher's *Seasons* and Pompadour, beyond the inscriptions and dedications of the Daullé prints, Nolhac has also suggested that the woman in the swan-decorated sleigh in *Winter* is a portrait of the marquise.[53] While her pretty features and elegant clothes cannot rule out a reference to the patron of the canvases, it seems unlikely that Boucher would have planned to include a portrait of Pompadour in the *Seasons*, as he never included portraits in his pastorals. Also unlikely is Nolhac's other suggestion (previously mentioned in a documentary source, in 1904) that the main nude woman in *Summer* is the Irish beauty Louise O'Murphy (1737–1814), known as La Belle Morphise, another of Louis XV's mistresses.[54] One of the denizens of the royal brothel of the Parc aux Cerfs and the king's lover between 1753 and 1755, Louise is said to have been used by Boucher as a model for some of his libertine paintings. It seems unlikely, however, that the painter would have included a portrait of her in a commission for Pompadour. The official mistress would have hardly appreciated the presence of a rival—albeit from a poor background and never presented at court—in paintings decorating her home.

The *Seasons* after Pompadour

Having struggled for years with bad health, Madame de Pompadour died at Versailles on April 15 (Palm Sunday), 1764. This was extraordinary, as no one except for members of the royal family were allowed to die in the chateau. Though she had been the king's devoted confidante for two decades, he was forbidden by protocol to be by her side at her death, after she was administered extreme unction. As Pompadour's body was carried from Versailles to Paris, where she was buried, the king stood on the balcony of his study and watched the hearse:

> He maintained a religious silence, watched the procession move along the avenue and, despite the bad weather and the cold air to which he seemed insensible, followed it with his eyes until it was entirely lost to view. He went back into his study; two large tears were running down his cheeks, and he

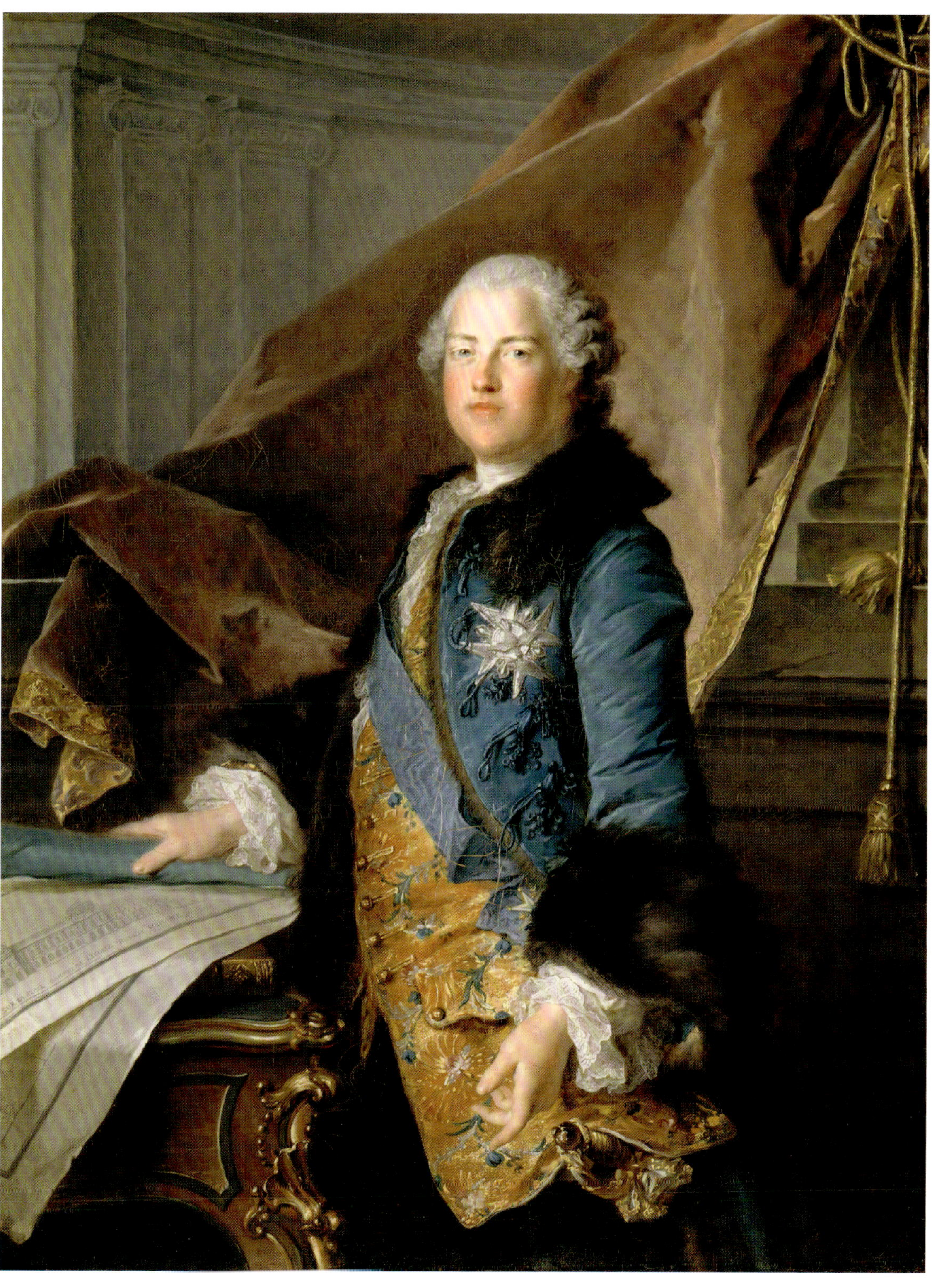

Fig. 39
Élisabeth-Louise Vigée Le Brun
Nicolas Beaujon, 1784
Pastel on paper
27 ¹⁵⁄₁₆ × 22 ¹³⁄₁₆ in. (71 × 58 cm)
Private collection

said only a few words to Champlost [his valet]: "Voilà les seul devoirs que j'aie pu rendre!" (Behold the only respects I can pay her!), the most eloquent words he could pronounce at that instant.[55]

Pompadour left her houses and collection to her young brother, Abel-François Poisson de Vandières, marquis de Menars et de Marigny (1727–1781) (fig. 38). The marquis de Marigny—as he was generally known—had been appointed *intendant général des bâtiments du roi* (minister of works) by the king in 1751. He maintained the title after the death of his sister and was a key figure in the art world in France in the mid-eighteenth century. After he died, a detailed inventory was compiled, in the summer of 1781, of the contents of his house in Paris—the Hôtel de Menars in Place des Victoires. The house had a long gallery for paintings, at the back, alongside the garden, and here the compiler of the inventory recorded: "850. Item four medium-sized, horizontal paintings, representing the seasons by F. Boucher and known through the prints by Daullé, canvas, value 500 *livres*."[56] Less than a year later, in February 1782, the collection of Marigny was up for auction in Paris; the sale took place "towards the end of February 1782, in his Hôtel, at Place des Victoires."[57] The sale catalogue describes the four canvases—as a single lot—in more detail: "[Boucher] 11. The Seasons in four paintings forming pendants. These subjects are known from the prints engraved by Daullé. Two of these paintings are pastorals; Summer is represented by women bathing and Winter by a lady in fur-trimmed robe in a sleigh pushed by a Tatar. On canvas, 27 *pouces* by 20 high."[58] They were purchased by a man called Vernier (probably an art dealer) for 1,402 *livres*.[59]

Boucher's *Seasons* seem to have changed hands quickly in the 1780s; by April 25, 1787, they were again on the market, this time in the estate sale of Nicolas Beaujon (1718–1786) (fig. 39), in Paris, who, coincidentally, had purchased Madame de Pompadour's Hôtel d'Evreux in 1773.[60] An extremely wealthy banker from Bordeaux, Beaujon had amassed a remarkable collection of paintings, including works by Peter Paul Rubens, Rembrandt, Frans Hals, Paolo Veronese, Adriaen van de Velde, Philips Wouwerman, Gerard Ter Borch, and Gerrit Dou and by contemporary French artists such as Boucher, Pater, Lancret, Jean-Baptiste Greuze, Antoine Coypel, and Jean Siméon Chardin, among others, as well as masterpieces such as Hans Holbein's *Ambassadors*, now in the National Gallery, London. At Beaujon's death, his collection was sold at auction at the Hôtel d'Evreux, and the four paintings went for 884

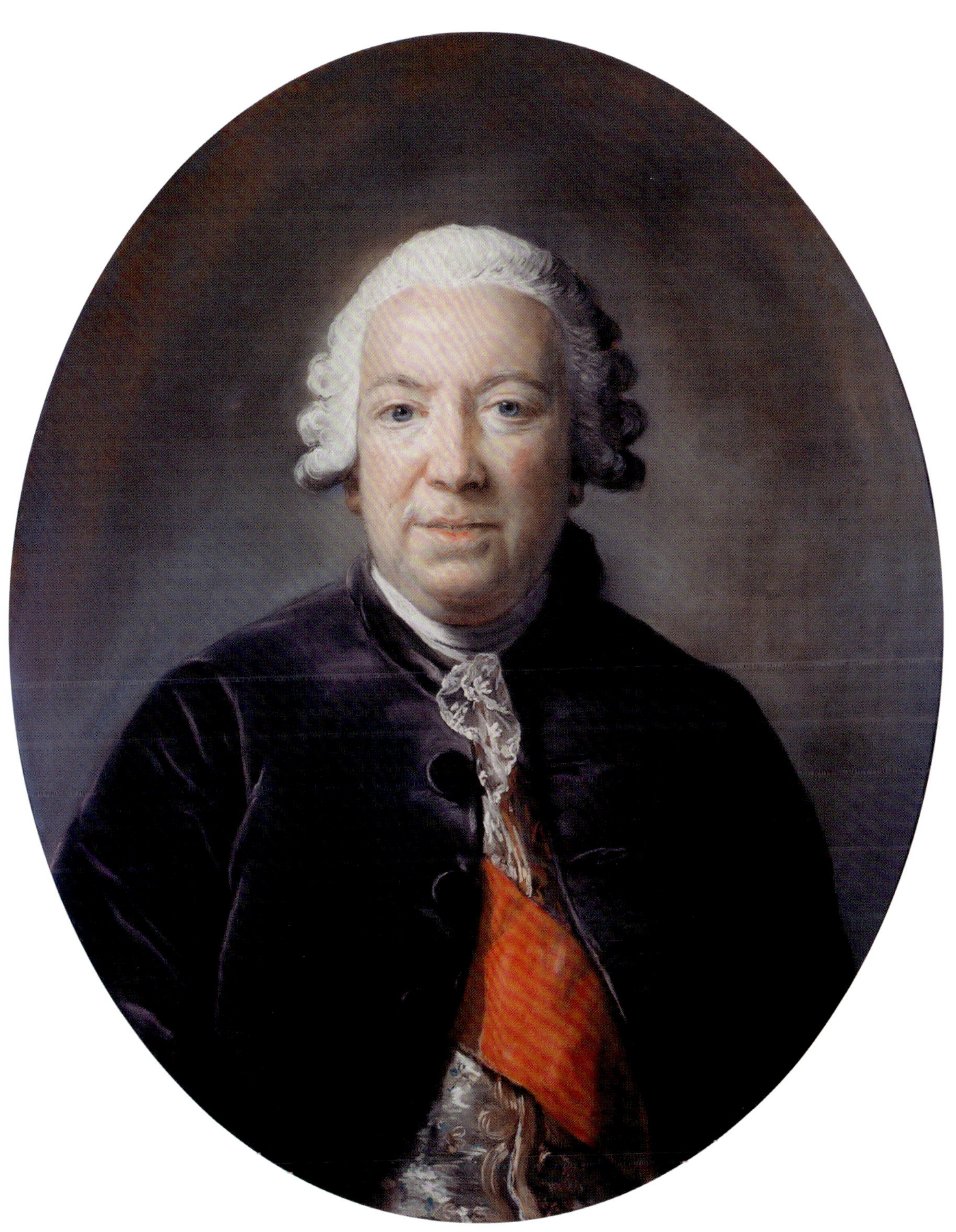

livres.[61] The buyer was recorded, in annotated sale catalogues, as "Remy," the art dealer Pierre Rémy (1715/16–1797).[62] Only a few years later, between April 28 and May 25, 1806, "four paintings representing the seasons" by Boucher appeared in the posthumous sale of the politician Vincent-Michel Maynon de Farceville (1716–1805).[63]

It is unclear where the *Seasons* were for almost seventy years, though they likely remained in Paris. In an exhibition in April 1874, at the Palais de la Présidence du Corps Législatif in Paris—an event organized to fundraise for the French colonization of Algeria—Boucher's *Four Seasons* were on view and lent by "M[onsieur] Ridgway."[64] Ten years later, in 1883–84, *The Four Seasons* were shown in an exhibition of eighteenth-century French art at the Galerie Georges Petit, in Paris, where they were also recorded as belonging to "M[onsieur] Ridgway."[65] Neither of the catalogues for these exhibitions expand on who Monsieur Ridgway was. The Galerie Georges Petit, which had hosted the exhibition in 1883–84, had a sale on December 3, 1904, of the possessions "following the death of Mme Ridgway," which included the four Boucher *Seasons*; each entry was accompanied by an illustration of the paintings.[66] Again, Madame Ridgway's full name is not included in the sale catalogue. A clue, however, is provided by a very short obituary in the *New York Times* on May 18, 1904, recording the death, the previous day, in Paris, of Elizabeth Ridgway, née Willing. From this, it is possible to suggest that "Monsieur Ridgway" was, most likely, John Jacob Ridgway (ca. 1807–1885), son of Jacob Ridgway (1768–1843), a merchant from Philadelphia who was American consul to Belgium in the early 1800s. John Jacob lived in Paris with his wife, Elizabeth. At his death, in 1885, his collection must have been inherited by his widow and put up for sale at the Galerie Georges Petit after her death. Little is known about John Jacob and Elizabeth Ridgway or how, when, and where they came into possession of *The Four Seasons*. It was in 1904, twelve years before Frick purchased the paintings from Virginia Bacon, that Eugène Fischhof bought the *Seasons* from the Ridgway sale and then sold them to Edward Rathbone Bacon.

*　*　*

Boucher's *Four Seasons* combine different modes of painting that would have been appreciated by a French eighteenth-century audience: the pastoral, the mythological, and the more straightforward genre scene. In this combination —

across four canvases—of different types of subjects typical of the times, collectors such as Edward Rathbone Bacon and Henry Clay Frick would have treasured perfect examples of Boucher's art made in 1755 for the most important patron in France after the king. Boucher's and Madame de Pompadour's love for the theater is clearly visible in the scenes depicted by the artist. Looking at the paintings is like looking at four different sets of a single theatrical performance.

The theatrical quality of the *Seasons* has been adopted, more recently, for the sets of a nineteenth-century Polish opera. In November 2015, a new production of *Straszny dwór* (The Haunted Manor), composed in 1861–64 by Stanisław Moniuszko (1819–1872), premiered at the Teatr Wielki—the Great Theatre—in Warsaw. A production by the Polish National Opera and directed by David Pountney, it included sets designed by Leslie Travers. The sets in the opera (fig. 40) were inspired by the Frick's *Four Seasons*, bringing to life the vignettes envisioned by the French painter in modern light boxes. The Warsaw sets bring back, full-circle, the *Seasons* from the theatrical productions in Madame de Pompadour's age, to Boucher's paintings, and back into today's world of the stage. The reason why the *Seasons* still capture the imagination is perfectly summarized by Mitford's characterization of their patron: "Madame de Pompadour excelled at an art which the majority of human beings thoroughly despise because it is unprofitable and ephemeral: the art of living."[67]

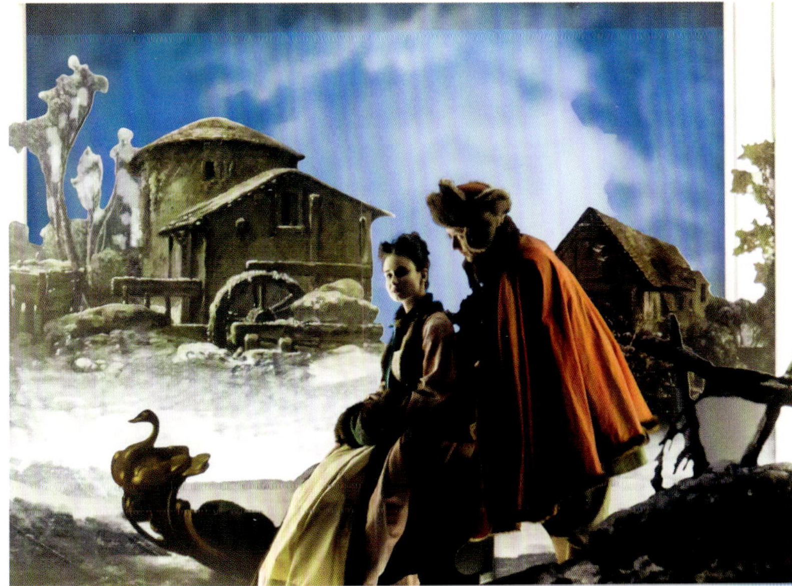

Fig. 40
Scene from Stanisław
Moniuszko's *Straszny dwór*
(The Haunted Manor)
Teatr Wielki, Warsaw

Notes

1 Letter from Virginia Bacon to Henry Clay Frick, September 30, 1916. Art Collecting Files of Henry Clay Frick. The Frick Collection/Frick Art Research Library Archives.

2 Ridgway sale 1904, 7–10, nos. 4–7.

3 Townsend and Howard 1919, 77–80.

4 Letter from Henry Clay Frick to Virginia Bacon, October 3, 1916. Art Collecting Files of Henry Clay Frick. The Frick Collection/Frick Art Research Library Archives.

5 For the Boucher Room, see E. Munhall in Davidson 1968, 8–23; and, most recently, Pullins 2022.

6 For the Fragonard Room, see Bailey 2011; Hollinghurst and Salomon 2022.

7 Art Collecting Files of Henry Clay Frick. The Frick Collection/Frick Art Research Library Archives.

8 Art Collecting Files of Henry Clay Frick. The Frick Collection/Frick Art Research Library Archives.

9 Art Collecting Files of Henry Clay Frick. The Frick Collection/Frick Art Research Library Archives.

10 For *The Four Seasons*, in general, see Goncourt 1880, 196; Mantz 1880, 122; Michel 1889, 98; Énault 1891; Nolhac 1905; Michel 1906, 88; Nolhac 1907, 75–78, 150; Nolhac 1925, 148–54; E. Munhall in Davidson 1968, 24–32; Ananoff 1976, 131; Ananoff 1980, 124, nos. 476–79; Brunel 1986, 286–87; Posner 1990, 96; Versailles, Munich, and London 2002–3, 238–41; Bailey 2004.

11 Delignières 1873, 75–79, nos. 102–5; Versailles, Munich, and London 2002–3, 238; Bailey 2004, 6.

12 Marquis de Menars sale 1782, 4.

13 For Boucher and his career, see Michel 1889; Michel 1906; Nolhac 1907; Nolhac 1925; Ananoff 1976; Ananoff 1980; Brunel 1986; New York, Detroit, and Paris 1986–87; London 2004–5; Hyde and Ledbury 2006; Pullins 2024.

14 For the series, see, most recently, L. Dalon in Versailles 2022–23, 278–83, nos. 124–32.

15 For the painting, see Faroult 2019.

16 For Boucher's work and different media, see, in particular, Pullins 2024.

17 For Boucher and tapestries, especially the "Tenture chinoise," see Besançon 2019–20.

18 Desprez 1768, 43.

19 For the two paintings, see Ingamells 1989, 61–63, 81–82, nos. P482, P489.

20 Jones 2002, 14.

21 Jones 2002, 84; H. Siefert in Versailles, Munich, and London 2002–3, 148–50, no. 27.

22 Albinson 2022, 31–35.

23 "d'une taille au-dessus de l'ordinaire, svelte, aisée, souple, élégante; son visage étoit bien assorti à sa taille, un ovale parfait, de beaux cheveux, plutôt châtain clair que blonds, des yeux assez grands, ornés de beaux sourcils de la même couleur, le nez perfaitement bien formé, la bouche charmante, . . . la plus belle peau du monde donnoit à tous ses traits le plus grand éclat. Ses yeux avoient un charme particulier, qu'ils devoient peut-être à l'incertitude de leur couleur; . . . l'ensemble de sa personne sembloit faire la nuance entre le dernier degré de l'élégance et le premier de la noblesse"; the description by Charles-Georges Leroy is published in Poulet-Malassis 1878, xxv–xxvi.

24 For Madame de Pompadour and her biography, see Mitford 2001; Jones 2002; Pevitt Algrant 2002; Craveri 2005, 296–327; Albinson 2022.

25 Mitford 2001, 138.

26 For Madame de Pompadour and the arts, see Posner 1990; Jones 2002; Versailles, Munich, and London 2002–3; London 2004–5, 99–129; Savill 2021; Albinson 2022.

27 Jones 2002, 150.

28 Mitford 2001, 167.

29 Mitford 2001, 159.

30 J. Hedley in London 2004–5, 99.

31 For the paintings, see R. Rand in Conisbee 2009, 19–25, no. 3; Baetjer 2019, 155–58, no. 41.

32 For the paintings and the king's bedroom at Bellevue, see Ingamells 1989, 68–78, nos. P485–P486; J. Hedley in London 2004–5, 104–15.

33 For the painting, see A. Laing in New York, Detroit, and Paris 1986–87, 244–48, no. 57.

34 The written restoration report is in the archives of the Conservation Department at The Frick Collection.

35 E. Munhall in Davidson 1968, 24.

36 For the paintings, see R. Rand in Conisbee 2009, 12–18, no. 2; Baetjer 2019, 151–55, no. 40.

37 For *chantourné* canvases, see, most recently, Pullins 2024, 145–80.

38 Pullins 2024, 146–48.

39 "Il donna ensuite à la célèbre Marquise quatre tableaux, représentant les quatre Saisons, et peignit plusieurs dessus de porte pour ses appartements"; Énault 1891. Also Nolhac 1925, 149; E. Munhall in Davidson 1968, 28.

40 "elles étaient destinées, à l'origine, à décorer une pièce élégante de dimensions moyennes, qui paraît s'être trouvée dans une des résidences de Madame de Pompadour"; Nolhac 1905, 2.

41 For the most complete accounts of Madame de
Pompadour's houses and their decoration, see Versailles,
Munich, and London 2002–3 and Savill 2021.

42 Cordey 1939.

43 Brunel 1986, 286.

44 Cordey 1939, 14, 26, 39, 61, 84, 87–93, 96.

45 "A l'égard de quatre dessus de porte, peints sur toile,
représentant différents sujets, ils n'ont point été prisés,
mais seullement tirée pour Mémoire"; Cordey 1939, 23.

46 Bailey 2004, 5.

47 Mitford 2001, 157.

48 "il trouva la nature fort désagréable, trop verte, mal
éclairée"; Houssaye 1843, 86.

49 M. Ledbury in Albinson 2022, 48.

50 "et toujours de persil sur les arbres"; Diderot 1795, 173.

51 For the influence of Watteau and Lancret, see Hazlehurst
1960; Brunel 1986, 287; Bailey 2004, 7.

52 J. Hedley in London 2004–5, 116–18.

53 Nolhac 1907, 76; Nolhac 1925, 151, 152.

54 Ridgway sale 1904, 8, no. 5; Nolhac 1905, 2; Nolhac
1907, 76; Townsend and Howard 1919, 78; Nolhac
1925, 151, 152.

55 Pevitt Algrant 2002, 288–89.

56 "850. Item quatre Moyens Tableaux en Travers
Representant Les Saisons par f. Boucher et Connus par
les gravures de Daullé Toile prise Cinq Cent Liv. 500";
Gordon 2003, 299.

57 "vers la fin de Février 1782, en son Hôtel, Place des
Victoires"; Marquis de Menars sale 1782.

58 "[Boucher] 11. Les Saisons en quatre Tableaux faisant
Pendants. Ces Sujets sont connus par les Estampes qu'en
a gravé Daullé. Deux de ces Tableaux sont des Pastorales;
l'Eté y est représenté par un bain de femmes, & l'hiver par
une Dame en robe bordée de poil, assise dans un traineau
poussé par un Tartare. T. 27 pouc. sur 20 de haut";
Marquis de Menars sale 1782, 4.

59 E. Munhall in Davidson 1968, 30.

60 For Beaujon, see Jeffares 2006, online edition [http://
www.pastellists.com/Essays/VigeeLeBrun_Beaujon.pdf
updated 22-04-2024].

61 Beaujeon sale 1787, 67, lot 202.

62 The annotated copy of the sale catalogue is in the
Bibliothèque de l'Institut National d'Histoire de l'Art,
collections Jacques Doucet, in Paris. The fact that the four
paintings were acquired in 1787 by "Ridgway" for 884
livres, as stated by Edgar Munhall (in Davidson 1968, 30)
is incorrect.

63 "[Boucher] Quatre Tableaux représentant les Saisons";
the dimensions ("Hauteur 20 pouces, largeur 26 pouc.")
match with the Frick *Seasons*; Maynon sale 1806, 82, lot
48.

64 Paris 1874, 13, nos. 25–28.

65 Paris 1883–84, 7, no. 12.

66 Ridgway sale 1904, 7–10, nos. 4–7.

67 Mitford 2001, 128.

BIBLIOGRAPHY

Albinson 2022 Albinson, A. Cassandra, ed. *Madame de Pompadour: Painted Pink*. Cambridge, MA, 2022.

Ananoff 1976 Ananoff, Alexandre. *François Boucher*. 2 vols. Lausanne and Paris, 1976.

Ananoff 1980 Ananoff, Alexandre. *L'opera completa di Boucher*. Milan, 1980.

Baetjer 2019 Baetjer, Katharine. *French Paintings in The Metropolitan Museum of Art from the Early Eighteenth Century through the Revolution*. New York, 2019.

Bailey 2004 Bailey, Colin B. "Pastorals and Genre Paintings: François Boucher's *Four Seasons*." *The Frick Collection Members' Magazine* (Spring/Summer 2004): 4–7.

Bailey 2011 Bailey, Colin B. *Fragonard's Progress of Love at The Frick Collection*. New York, 2011.

Beaujeon sale 1787 *Catalogue de tableaux, marbres, bronzes, porcelaines, lustres, girandoles, feux, pendules & autres objets distingués après le décès de M. Beaujeon*. Sale cat. Hôtel d'Evreux, Paris, April 25, 1787.

Besançon 2019–20 Yohan Rimaud, ed. *Une des provinces du rococo: La Chine rêvée de François Boucher*. Exh. cat. Besançon (Musée des Beaux-Arts et d'Archéologie), 2019–20.

Brunel 1986 Brunel, Georges. *Boucher*. Paris and New York, 1986.

Conisbee 2009 Conisbee, Philip, ed. *French Paintings of the Fifteenth through the Eighteenth Century. National Gallery of Art, Washington*. Washington, DC, 2009.

Cordey 1939 Cordey, Jean. *Inventaire des biens de Madame de Pompadour rédigé après son décès*. Paris, 1939.

Craveri 2005 Craveri, Benedetta. *Amanti e regine: Il potere delle donne*. Milan, 2005.

Davidson 1968 Davidson, Bernice, et al. *The Frick Collection: An Illustrated Catalogue*. Vol. 2, *Paintings: French, Italian and Spanish*. New York, 1968.

Delignières 1873 Delignières, Émile. *Catalogue raisonné de l'oeuvre gravé de Jean Daullé d'Abbeville précédé d'une notice sur sa vie et ses ouvrages*. Paris, 1873.

Desprez 1768 Desprez, Guillaume-Nicolas. *Le Nécrologe des hommes célèbres de France*. Paris, 1768.

Énault 1891 Énault, Louis. *D'après François Boucher*. Paris, 1891.

Faroult 2019 Faroult, Guillaume. *François Boucher: L'Odalisque brune*. Paris, 2019.

Goncourt 1880 Goncourt, Edmond and Jules. *L'Art du dix-huitième siècle*. Paris, 1880.

Gordon 2003 Gordon, Alden R. *The Houses and Collections of the Marquis de Marigny*. Los Angeles, 2003.

Hazlehurst 1960 Hazlehurst, F. Hamilton. "The Origins of a Boucher Theme." *Gazette des Beaux-Arts* 55 (1960): 109–16.

Hollinghurst and Salomon 2022 Hollinghurst, Alan, and Xavier F. Salomon. *Fragonard's Progress of Love*. New York and London, 2022.

Houssaye 1843 Houssaye, Arsène. "Boucher et la peinture sous Louis XV." *Revue des Deux Mondes* 3 (July 1843): 70–98.

Hyde and Ledbury 2006 Hyde, Melissa, and Mark Ledbury, eds. *Rethinking Boucher*. Los Angeles, 2006.

Ingamells 1989 Ingamells, John. *The Wallace Collection Catalogue of Pictures*. Vol. 3, *French before 1815*. London, 1989.

Jeffares 2006 Jeffares, Neil. *Dictionary of Pastellists before 1800*. Norwich, 2006. Online edition, 2010 [http://www.pastellists.com].

Jones 2002 Jones, Colin. *Madame de Pompadour: Images of a Mistress*. London, 2002.

London 2004–5 Jo Hedley, ed. *François Boucher: Seductive Visions*. Exh. cat. London (The Wallace Collection), 2004–5.

Mantz 1880 Mantz, Paul. *François Boucher, Lemoyne et Natoire*. Paris, 1880.

Marquis de Menars sale 1782 *Catalogue des différens objets de curiosités dans les sciences et arts qui composoient le cabinet de feu M. le Marquis de Menars*. Sale cat. Hôtel de Menars, Paris, February 1782.

Michel 1889 Michel, André. *F. Boucher*. Paris, 1889.

Michel 1906 Michel, André. *François Boucher*. Paris, 1906.

Mitford 2001 Mitford, Nancy. *Madame de Pompadour*. New York, 2001.

New York, Detroit, and Paris 1986–87 Alastair Laing, J. Patrice Marandel, and Pierre Rosenberg, eds. *François Boucher, 1703–1770*. Exh. cat. New York (Metropolitan Museum of Art), Detroit (Detroit Institute of Arts), and Paris (Grand Palais), 1986–87.

Nolhac 1905 Nolhac, Pierre de. "'Les Quatre Saisons' de François Boucher." *Les Arts* 39 (1905): 2–7.

Nolhac 1907 Nolhac, Pierre de. *François Boucher, premier peintre du roi, 1703–1770*. Paris, 1907.

Nolhac 1925 Nolhac, Pierre de. *Boucher, premier peintre du roi*. Paris, 1925.

Paris 1874 *Explication des ouvrages de peinture exposés au profit de la colonisation de l'Algérie par les Alsaciens-Lorrains*. Exh. cat. Paris (Palais de la Présidence du Corps Législatif), 1874.

Paris 1883–84 *L'Art au XVIIIᵉ siècle*. Exh. cat. Paris (Galerie Georges Petit), 1883–84.

Pevitt Algrant 2002 Pevitt Algrant, Christine. *Madame de Pompadour: Mistress of France*. London, 2002.

Posner 1990 Posner, Donald. "Mme de Pompadour as a Patron of the Visual Arts." *Art Bulletin* 72 (1990): 74–105.

Poulet-Malassis 1878 Poulet-Malassis, Auguste, ed. *Correspondance de Mme de Pompadour*. Paris, 1878.

Pullins 2022 Pullins, David. "A Boucher Room. Medium, Time, and Authorship." In *L'Art de l'Ancien Régime: Sortir du rang!*, edited by Tomas Kirchner, Sophie Raux, and Marlen Schneider, 71–86. Heidelberg, 2022.

Pullins 2024 Pullins, David. *The Mobile Image from Watteau to Boucher*. Los Angeles, 2024.

Ridgway sale 1904 *Catalogue de tableaux anciens et modernes, quatre remarquables peintures de Fr. Boucher de l'ancienne collection de la Marquise de Pompadour et oeuvres de Bachelier, Blin de Fontenay, Callet, Charpentier, Demarne, Leriche, H. Robert, J. Vernet, Louis Watteau etc., gravures de l'École française des XVIIᵉ et XVIIIᵉ siècles, objets d'art et d'ameublement . . . dont la vente, par suite du décès de Mme Ridgway*. Sale cat. Galerie Georges Petit, Paris, December 3, 1904.

Savill 2021 Savill, Rosalind. *Everyday Rococo: Madame de Pompadour and Sèvres Porcelain*. 2 vols. London, 2021.

Townsend and Howard 1919 Townsend, James B., and W. Stanton Howard. *Memorial Catalogue of Paintings by Old and Modern Masters Collected by Edward R. Bacon*. New York, 1919.

Versailles 2022–23 Yves Carlier and Hélène Delalex, eds. *Louis XV: Passions d'un roi, 1710–1774*. Exh. cat. Versailles (Châteaux de Versailles), 2022–23.

Versailles, Munich, and London 2002–3 Xavier Salmon, ed. *Madame de Pompadour et les arts*. Exh. cat. Versailles (Musée National des Châteaux de Versailles et de Trianon), Munich (Kunsthalle der Hypo-Kulturstiftung), and London (National Gallery), 2002–3.

IMAGE CREDITS

Photographs have been provided by the owners or custodians of the works. The following list applies to those photographs for which a separate credit is due.

Figs. 3, 5, 7, 9, 11, 14, 30; pages 12–19: Joseph Coscia Jr.

Figs. 6, 8, 10, 12, 13, 16, 19, 23, 24, 29, 38: © RMN-Grand Palais / Art Resource, NY

Fig. 15: Pushkin Museum, Moscow / Bridgeman Images

Figs. 17, 18: Centre Historique des Archives Nationales, Paris / Bridgeman Images

Figs. 20, 21, 27, 28: © Wallace Collection, London / Bridgeman Images

Fig. 22: Bavarian State Painting Collections - Alte Pinakothek Munich

Fig. 31: Courtesy Frick Art Research Library

Figs. 34–37: Château de Fontainebleau, Seine-et-Marne, France / Bridgeman Images

Fig. 40: Photo Krzysztof Bieliński